THE BEST PODCASTS

The Secret Formula
For Enjoying Podcasts

KRIS BALLARD

THE BEST PODCASTS
Copyright © 2022 by Kris Ballard

TABLE OF CONTENTS

DEDICATION

This book is dedicated to David Ballard.
Not only is he my brother, but he is also my friend.

INTRODUCTION

This book will help you find interesting podcasts to listen to. In fact, it will introduce you to a dozen different podcasts. Thankfully, the podcasts are both informative and entertaining.

In other words, the podcasts I am asking you to listen to won't be a waste of your time. Indeed, these podcasts are shows I enjoy listening to. Since I'm a writer, though, the first few shows will be about writing and self-publishing.

Then, for a change of pace, I will tell you about the *James Altucher Show.* For those who don't know, the *James Altucher Show* is a podcast about a wide variety of topics. So, give this podcast a try. I know you're going to love it.

Another fascinating podcast is called the *Remarkable People* podcast. This podcast is hosted by Guy Kawasaki, and like the title says, he has remarkable people on his show. Although Kawasaki is new to podcasting, he has already created quite a few episodes.

Someone else with a great podcast is Matt Nappo. The podcast Nappo hosts is called the *MinddogTV* podcast. Although I hadn't heard of Nappo until recently, I'm certainly glad I discovered his podcast.

The nice thing about podcasts is that it makes it easy to listen to amazing interviews. In fact, since I enjoy listening to podcasts, I decided to create my own show. For those who are interested, my podcast is called *Ballard's Book Coaching* Podcast. As the title suggests, my podcast is focused on writing.

Indeed, after reading this book, you might also be interested in starting a podcast. However, this book is primarily designed to tell you about the amazing podcasts you can listen to. So, now that you know what this book is about, it's time for you to learn about the best podcasts.

CHAPTER 1
THE CREATIVE PENN

For those who think they would like to write a book, The *Creative Penn* is the podcast for you. I have learned a lot from this podcast over the past few years. So, let me tell you a little bit more about this informative show.

The host of *The Creative Penn*, is Joanna Penn. Not only does Penn host her own podcast, but she is also an author. Indeed, Penn writes both nonfiction and fiction books. I have read some of Penn's nonfiction books, and they are excellent.

Since Penn has been writing for a while, she is worth listening to. I must warn you, though, most episodes on her weekly podcast are about an hour long. In other words, you will need to set aside some time if you want to listen to an episode.

Something else to be aware of is that Joanna Penn has already recorded hundreds of podcast episodes. This is great because you will be able to listen to some of her earlier episodes. However, don't be discouraged if you don't have time to listen to all the episodes.

Instead, be grateful the podcasts are high-quality. I suggest starting out by only listening to the podcast episodes that seem to be the most interesting.

Before we go any further, let me mention that there are many places on the Internet where you can listen to podcasts. The most obvious place to begin with, though, is by looking for the podcaster's website.

For example, type *The Creative Penn* podcast into your favorite search engine. When you do this, at the top of the list you will find a link to *The Creative Penn*. Then, when you click on this link, you will find yourself on *The Creative Penn* website.

In fact, you will be on the podcast section of the website. So, scroll through the podcast episodes and then decide which episodes you want to listen to. Of course, since there are so many good episodes, it will be difficult to decide.

However, if you don't want to listen to podcast episodes directly from this website, then listen to them on Stitcher or Spotify. If for some reason you don't like Stitcher or Spotify, then look for a podcasting website you do like.

The point I'm making, is there are a variety of different ways to listen to podcasts. So, find out what works for you. I want podcasts to inform and entertain you.

Now, let's get back to talking about *The Creative Penn*. As I said previously, the episodes on this podcast are lengthy.

To be honest, I wish they were a bit shorter. Overall, though, I'm impressed with *The Creative Penn* podcast.

In a typical episode, Joanna Penn begins by speaking for about twenty minutes. During this part of the show, she lets you know about the latest developments in the self-publishing world. Since Penn is an experienced writer, it's makes sense to listen to her advice.

Afterwards, she will interview a guest. This is the part of her show I especially enjoy. Thankfully, all the guests on *The Creative Penn* are people who know what they are talking about.

Interestingly enough, Penn doesn't always agree with everything her guests say. She doesn't do this to be disagreeable, though. Rather, she wants to share her knowledge with her listeners.

So, now that you have a general idea of what to expect, let me tell you about my favorite episodes. Indeed, I'm going to start by telling you about episode #378. This episode is titled: "Strangers To Superfans". This title may sound confusing until you realize this is also the title of a book.

David Gaughran is not only the author of this book, but he is also the guest on this podcast episode. The first thing you will notice about this episode is that Gaughran has an Irish accent. Fortunately, though, he is easy to understand.

The reason Joanna Penn has this fellow on her show is because she wants to learn about his book marketing methods. Althoughhe Gaughran is quite knowledgeable about book marketing, he certainly isn't arrogant.

In fact, he spends most of the episode joking around about all the mistakes he has made. One thing Gaughran suggests is that writers need to learn more about email marketing. For those who don't know, email marketing is a great way to market your books.

Indeed, after listening to Gaughran, I now want to read some of his books. As you listen to podcast episodes on *The Creative Penn*, you might also become fascinated with some of the guests.

Now, let's look at another podcast episode that's available on *The Creative Penn*. In episode #314, Joanna Penn interviews Jerod Morris. I'm glad she does since he is a podcasting expert.

So, if you're thinking about starting a podcast, this is a good episode to listen to. One question many beginning podcasters have is, "What kind of equipment do I need?" In fact, as a beginning podcaster, this is something I'm trying to figure out.

Morris thinks doesn't think beginners should buy expensive podcasting equipment. The reason he says this is because not every beginning podcaster is going to enjoy interviewing people.

Later, though, after you decide that podcasting really is for you, go ahead and buy some expensive equipment. Joanna

Penn agrees with this advice since she started her own podcast with some very basic equipment.

Obviously, though, not every author needs to start a podcast. However, don't be surprised if a podcast host asks you to be a guest on their show. In other words, you need to learn a little bit about podcasting.

Let me tell you about another podcast episode. In episode #414, Penn interviews Tammy Labrecque about email marketing. To be honest, this episode was especially interesting to me.

You are probably wondering, "How can email marketing be interesting?" In fact, in the old days, I would have agreed with you. Recently, though, I have become very interested in email marketing since it is a priority for me.

Thankfully, Labrecque literally wrote the book on email marketing. In case you're curious, her book is titled: *Newsletter Ninja*. I bought the eBook version of *Newsletter Ninja* and I'm reading it now.

Labrecque has also written other books besides *Newsletter Ninja*. For instance, she has written many books for the romance genre. Some of her books were written under different pen names.

Since email marketing is something many writers struggle with, Labrecque's insights are extremely valuable. One good point she makes is that writing email newsletters should be fun. So, if writing email messages to your readers is making you miserable, then you're not doing it the right way.

Not only was I impressed with Tammy Lebrecque, but Joanna Penn also learned a lot from her. So, I encourage you to listen to this particular episode. Indeed, if email marketing is something you haven't thought much about, now is the time to start thinking about it.

Now, for a change of pace, let's learn about writing retreats. In episode #451, Penn interviews Jen Louden. I enjoyed learning from Louden because she has been working at this writing thing for a while.

In fact, back in the day, she was even interviewed by Oprah Winfrey. The interesting thing, though, is that Louden became depressed after the interview because she realized she was spending too much time looking for approval from other people.

However, eventually Louden discovered that she didn't need anyone else to give her permission to accomplish big things. It was a hard lesson for her to learn, but learning this about herself, made Louden a stronger person.

Now, den is helping other writers with her writing retreats. Indeed, her writing retreats have become quite popular. Joanna Penn asked Louden if she had advice for writers who can't afford to attend writing retreats.

Louden says that there are alternatives. For example, when Louden wasn't making much progress with her writing, she stayed in a cabin for five days. Thankfully, there weren't any distractions at the cabin, so Louden was able to write thousands of words.

For most writers, though, they just need to let their family know they need some quiet time. Although, if you're new to writing, it may take some time for your family to get used to your writing routine.

As you can see, Jen Louden is an interesting person who has also been writing books for a while. So, if you want to get some good advice from an experienced writer, then listen to this podcast episode.

Hopefully, by now you're beginning to see how useful *The Creative Penn* podcast is for writers. In fact, even if you aren't a writer, you will still find a lot of helpful advice in this podcast.

The next episode, which I will be describing to you, is an interview with Amanda Brown. For those who want to listen to this interview, it's episode #463. The first thing you will notice while you're listening to Brown is that she has a British accent. Although Joanna Penn also has a British accent, it's not as noticeable as Brown's.

Brown hasn't written very many books. This is alright, though, because she is an expert on the business side of writing. The reason Brown knows so much about business is because she started her career in the financial world.

However, when Brown became a mother, she decided she wanted to work from home. Fortunately, this turned out to be a good decision. Now, even though her children are adults, Brown continues to work for herself.

Since many people want to learn how to work for themselves, Brown's advice is valuable. Unfortunately, though, many writers don't know much about financial matters. Of course, this isn't good, because then these writers won't have the money they need.

This is why you need to educate yourself about the business side of writing. Although you might not be making much money right now, you still need to plan for the future. So, even if you're a new writer, it makes sense to listen to Amanda Brown.

Now that we have talked about money, it's time to talk about publicity. In podcast episode #452, Joanna Penn interviews Dana Kaye. For those who don't know, Kaye is an expert in gaining publicity for writers.

In fact, Kaye knows so much about publicity that she has written a book on this topic. Since you may not have enough money to hire a publicist, you should listen to this podcast episode.

I'd also like to suggest that you buy Kaye's eBook entitled *Your Book, Your Brand*. The reason I suggest this is because you're capable of becoming your own publicist.

Right now, you're probably thinking, "I don't want to be a publicist, I just want to write books." To be honest, I feel the same way. However, sometimes we need to move past our feelings to get things done.

If you don't mind spending a lot of money, though, you can hire Kaye to help you. This might sound like a good option until you realize Kaye is already working with a lot of clients. In other words, you will probably be put on a waiting list.

Sadly, this chapter is almost over. The good news, though, is that Joanna Penn has hundreds of podcast episodes for you to listen to. Indeed, there are many episodes I still need to listen to.

Now, though, it's time for chapter two. In the second chapter, you will learn about another podcast I think you will enjoy listening to. Are you ready?

CHAPTER 2
THE SELF-PUBLISHING SHOW

First of all, let me begin by saying that *The Self-Publishing Show* is similar to *The Creative Penn* podcast. In fact, the man who created *The Self-Publishing Show*, Mark Dawson, happens to be Joanna Penn's close friend. Although Dawson created the podcast, he has a co-host named James Blatch who is actually the one who interviews people for the podcast.

Something I like about Dawson's podcast is that you can watch it on YouTube. Somehow, it adds an extra dimension when you are able to watch the podcast. However, I do wish Dawson would also interview some of the guests. Thankfully, though, his co-host is brilliant at interviewing people.

Let's look at episode #199 so that you can learn a little bit about *The Self-Publishing Show*. In this episode, Blatch interviews Sarah Painter. Interestingly enough, Painter had a tough time learning how to write books.

Sadly, for many years, Painter didn't think she was capable of writing. Not only that, but even the thought of writing frightened Painter. For some reason, she thought that only unusually gifted people were allowed to be writers.

Fortunately, though, Painter eventually learned how to overcome her writing fears. Indeed, writing is now her full-time job. This doesn't mean she never feels anxious about her writing. Now, though, she doesn't let her fears prevent her from writing books.

Since Painter conquered many of her writing fears, she wants to help other writers. Of course, not every writer is going to face the same challenges as Painter. For example, my biggest challenge as a beginning writer was feeling self-conscious about my punctuation.

However, even if your writing challenges are different than Painter's, I'm still going to encourage you to listen to this podcast episode.

Now, though, it's time to learn about a different author. In episode #169, James Blatch interviews Alessandra Torre. In this episode you will learn that Torre is a romance writer. Although Torre is a successful author, she realizes she has made some mistakes along the way.

One of the biggest mistakes she made was signing with a traditional publisher. The reason she made this mistake was because the publisher offered her a lot of money. Right now, you're probably wondering, "How can making a lot of money be bad?"

To make a long story short, Torre would have made more money if she had self-published her book. In fact, Torre wishes she could buy back the rights for the three books she sold to this publisher. The reason Torre doesn't buy back her rights, though, is because it would probably cost $200,000.

Although Torre has made some business mistakes with her writing, she still hasn't had to go back to her day job. Indeed, Torre makes a good income from the books she writes. However, Torre cautions writers to be careful about the contracts they sign.

Something else Torre talks about in this interview is a writer's conference she organized. Unfortunately, since this interview took place a few years ago, it's too late to attend the conference.

Although I have never felt the need to attend a writer's conference, Torre is enthusiastic about them. The reason she loves writer's conferences is because they offer an opportunity for networking. Also, Torre believes these conferences are informative.

If you're not able to attend a writer's conference in person, don't worry, because you can usually attend them over the Internet. To be honest, that's how I would attend a conference, but that might be because I happen to be a hermit, so you might want to do things differently.

Guess what? It's time to learn about another podcast guest. In episode #232, James Blatch interviews Vicky Fraser. Believe it or not, Fraser was interviewed because she bribed Mark Dawson and James Blatch with a basket full of delicious treats.

Thankfully, though, Fraser knows a lot about writing. Not only does she write nonfiction books, but she also encourages other people to write. However, if you're going to write, Fraser thinks you should write something people will want to read.

But many beginning writers are intimidated at the thought of writing an interesting nonfiction book. Fraser believes the way to make your writing interesting is by telling stories.

In other words, if done the right way, a nonfiction book can be just as exciting as a novel. Unfortunately, though, many nonfiction authors never learn the importance of storytelling. Of course, James Blatch agreed with Fraser's writing advice and to support it, he mentioned some of his favorite nonfiction books.

There's something else interesting about Fraser. She knows a lot about copywriting. For those who don't know what copywriting is, it's a type of persuasive writing. In fact, the main purpose of copywriting is to get people to buy things.

Since writers need people to buy their books, they need to learn about this topic. Indeed, if you are a writer, then you need to learn about copywriting.

The main takeaway from this interview, though, is that nonfiction writers should write books that people will want to read. So, if you want to write an amazing nonfiction book, then this is the podcast episode you should listen to.

The next podcast episode I think you should listen to is an interview with Jane Friedman. For those who want to listen to this podcast, it's episode #285. Although Friedman hasn't written many books, she happens to be an expert on the publishing industry.

Thankfully, Friedman is knowledgeable about both traditional publishing and self-publishing. Even though her background is in traditional publishing, Friedman is impressed with what self-publishers are doing.

According to Friedman, self-publishers are more experimental with the way they market their books. For example, most self-publishers are happy to sell their books in the eBook format. Although selling eBooks may sound like a sensible thing to do, traditional publishers hate eBooks.

You might be wondering why. Well, the biggest reason is because they are stuck in the past. Indeed, even though eBooks have been available for a while, traditional publishers still haven't gotten used to them.

However, although, the big publishers make a lot of mistakes, they don't do everything wrong. In fact, Friedman believes that self-publishers can learn from traditional publishers. Of course, the best way to learn from self-publishers is to look for examples of when they brilliantly promoted a book.

Personally, though, I think Friedman should be more critical of traditional publishers. Sadly, in the past, huge publishers have been the gatekeepers that prevented books from being published.

Although I have gone on a bit of a rant, I still believe Jane Friedman's advice is valuable. In fact, I have even signed up for her paid newsletter. For those who don't know, Friedman's newsletter is called The Hot Sheet.

So, if you want to keep up with what's going on in the publishing industry, The Hot Sheet is a great resource. Thankfully, your first two newsletters will be free. After that you will need to pay for them.

If you haven't yet written a book, I hope you will consider writing one. Indeed, I hope you will consider writing several books. Although writing a book isn't easy, it's not nearly as hard as you might think.

Unfortunately, marketing your book is more difficult than writing it. This is why podcasts such as *The Self-Publishing Show* are so important for writers to listen to. However, now it's time to learn about IngramSpark.

Unless you already know a lot about publishing, you have probably never heard of IngramSpark. That's alright, though, because in episode #278, Sara Rosett will tell you why she likes IngramSpark.

For those who don't know, IngramSpark is a company that can help you self-publish your books. Sadly, when Rosett first started writing, it was difficult for authors to self-publish their books. So, instead of self-publishing her books, Rosett published her books with a traditional publisher.

This turned out to be a mistake, though, because Rossett's publisher didn't properly market her books. Although Rosett wishes she could get back the rights to those books, her old publisher won't allow her to do this.

The reason why her publisher won't let Rosett have the rights to her books is because they are making money from them. Rosett doesn't tell you this because she wants you to feel sorry for her. Instead, she mentions this so that you won't make the same mistakes she made.

Now Rosett self-publishes her books. This is great because it allows her to own the rights to her books. Also, when she self-publishes her books, Rosett makes a lot more money. So whenever traditional publishers offer to publish her books, Rosett politely declines.

During this interview, James Blatch was impressed with Rosett's knowledge. Indeed, she knows quite a bit about self-publishing. When Rosett is self-publishing her books, she uses IngramSpark. Since she has had success with IngramSpark, she wants to teach other writers about this company.

Since, I have only self-published one of my books with IngramSpark, I really enjoyed learning from Sara Rosett. One of the things Rosett explains is that IngramSpark is based on a wholesale model rather than the retail model Amazon uses. Since most authors are familiar with Amazon's model, the wholesale model can confuse authors.

However, if you're interested in selling your books to bookstores and libraries, then IngramSpark is the better option. In fact, most bookstores and libraries won't order books from Amazon. In other words, it doesn't make sense for Barnes and Noble to order books from their rival.

So, if you want to see your books in bookstores, you will need to learn about IngramSpark. Indeed, a good place to start your education on this topic is by listening to Rosett. You will be glad you did.

Now, it's time to learn about Audiobooks. In episode #220, James Blatch interviews Joanna Penn whose podcast we learned quite a bit about in the first chapter of this book. This time, though, she will be the guest, instead of the host.

In this interview you will quickly learn that Penn enjoys the technological side of writing. In fact, back when podcasts were quite primitive, she already had her own podcast. What Blatch wants to know about, though, is audiobooks.

Fortunately, Penn is happy to tell him about audiobooks since she has written a book on this topic. One of the things Penn likes about audiobooks is that they are becoming very popular with readers. Indeed, every year more people are listening to audiobooks.

There is a lot, though, which goes into creating an audiobook. For example, you will need to decide if you want to narrate your own book. Although Penn narrates her books, some authors prefer to hire a narrator.

However, be aware that it costs a lot of money to hire a narrator. The reason narrators charge so much is because narrating a book is hard work. So, if you want a talented narrator to work for you, you will need to pay them.

In the future, though, things might be different. In fact, it's already possible to synthesize voices. In other words, there are companies than can create a computerized version of your voice. Indeed, Penn believes people should be allowed to license their voices.

As you can see in this interview with Joanna Penn, she studies technological trends. Now it's time to learn about a different type of podcast, so let's get started.

CHAPTER 3
THE JAMES ALTUCHER SHOW

The James Altucher Show is a podcast that covers many different topics. Normally I like to listen to a podcast that is focused on a single topic. With this particular podcast, though, I'm willing to make an exception.

I suggest you listen to Altucher's podcast on the Stitcher website. At least that's the website I use for listening to his show.

When you look at a picture of James Altucher, the first thing you notice is all his curly hair. Although his hair is fascinating, his podcast is where you will learn new things.

The best way for you to understand what his podcast is about is for me to describe some of the episodes. Let's start with episode #733. In this episode, Altucher interviews Mike Rothschild about QAnon.

For those who don't know, QAnon is a conspiracy theory which many people believe in. Unfortunately, the people who believe in QAnon are believing in something that isn't true.

Rothschild is an expert on QAnon. Indeed, he has even written a book on this topic. Since Rothschild is knowledgeable about QAnon, Altucher wanted to talk to him.

In case you're curious, Mike Rothschild isn't related to the wealthy Rothschild's family. Rothschild wishes he was, though, so he wouldn't have to work so hard. Instead, he is a man who spends his time debunking conspiracy theories.

Unfortunately, because of Rothchild's last name, many conspiracy theorists think he is a bad man. Indeed, because of his last name, it would be impossible for Rothschild to properly interview members of QAnon.

Although believing in QAnon might seem harmless, some of its members are violent. This is why you need to be careful when you are talking to someone who believes in this particular conspiracy theory.

It can be heartbreaking, though, if you have a family member who believes in QAnon. Of course, James Altucher was fascinated with QAnon and his knowledgeable guest. To be honest, I also learned some things about QAnon that I didn't know.

The main takeaway from this interview, though, is that QAnon is a conspiracy theory which needs to be taken seriously. I agree with Rothschild on this. The reason I agree with him is because I have a dear friend who was led astray by QAnon.

Indeed, when people tried to convince my friend that QAnon wasn't true, she still stubbornly believed in it. Hopefully, though, you don't have a friend or family member who has been brainwashed by conspiracy theories. But if you do, I suggest listening to this podcast episode.

Now, for a change of pace, let's learn about the business world. In episode #719, James Altucher interviews John Lee Dumas. For those who don't know, Dumas is a very talented entrepreneur.

Although Dumas and Altucher are friends, these two men have very different personalities. For example, Dumas has made quite a bit of money by not allowing himself to get distracted. In other words, Dumas doesn't jump from one idea to the next.

Indeed, Dumas became successful in the business world by creating his own podcast. For those who are curious, his podcast is called Entrepreneurs on Fire. Since Dumas creates a new podcast episode every day, he now has nearly 3,000 episodes.

Many people enjoy listening to Dumas's podcast because they want to learn how to become an entrepreneur. Some of the people who listen to his podcast, though, are already entrepreneurs. This makes sense, because even successful people want to learn new things.

When people listen to the Entrepreneurs on Fire podcast, they are able to listen to interesting and informative interviews. Of course, Dumas only interviews the most talented entrepreneurs on his show.

Although many people think Dumas is creative, he doesn't think of himself this way. In fact, Dumas believes that the only creative idea he ever had was to create his podcast. Personally, I believe Dumas is being modest when he says this.

However, there is some truth to what he says since all his other business ideas are similar to his podcast. One idea Dumas had was to create a special journal for his listeners. Of course, many people wanted to buy his journal, so he made a lot of money from this product.

Since James Altucher has trouble staying focused, he really admires John Lee Dumas. In my opinion, though, Dumas is a little bit too focused. In other words, I think Altucher is fine by just being himself.

If you are interested in learning more about Dumas, I will be talking about him in the next chapter. Now, though, it's time to learn about physics. In episode #717, James Altucher interviews Michio Kaku. Believe it or not, I have known about Kaku for a long time.

Of course, I don't know him personally, but I have seen his books in libraries and bookstores. In addition to this, I have also seen interviews with Kaku on the Internet. In other words, Kaku is kind of a big deal.

Interestingly enough, you can still enjoy this interview even if you don't know very much about physics. The reason for this is that Kaku knows how to simplify complicated concepts. He has studied physics for a very long time. In fact, when he was only eight years old, Michio Kaku became interested in physics. He is also interested in science fiction.

Indeed, Kaku likes to speculate about some far-out ideas and concepts. Of course, many of Kaku's physicist friends can't figure out why he is fascinated with science fiction movies and books. He doesn't really care if his friends roll their eyes, though, because Kaku happens to love science fiction.

Although he has a fun-loving side, Kaku is also an important physicist. In fact, Kaku was one of the physicists who created string theory. For those who don't know, string theory is an exciting new way to look at physics.

Right now, you're probably wondering, "What does a string have to do with physics?" That's a good question. Kaku believes the universe was created with tiny little vibrating strings. In other words, music created the universe.

Personally, I hope string theory is true because it would answer many important questions. Many physicists, though, don't like string theory. Instead, they believe in a theory called the Standard Model.

Of course, the Standard Model isn't beautiful. In fact, it's rather ugly. However, many physicists still prefer the Standard Model. Although I'm not a physicist, I have always been attracted to string theory. For some reason, it just seems to make more sense to me.

Even if you have never been interested in science, though, I still encourage you to listen to this interview. Indeed, it will take you less than an hour to listen to it, and you will be glad you did.

It's time now to learn about innovation. In episode #590, Altucher interviews Matt Ridley. Since Ridley is one of Altucher's favorite authors, he was excited to interview him. In fact, Altucher had been trying to interview Ridley for six years.

Thankfully, Altucher and Ridley were finally able to discuss the subject of innovation. Probably the best example of innovation was when the Wright Brothers invented the airplane. Although other people tried to invent the airplane, it was the Wright Brothers who were successful.

Since, Ridley is a deep thinker, he has spent a lot of time trying to learn more about the Wright Brothers. Indeed, the reason Ridley researched the Wright Brothers is because he enjoys learning about innovative people.

Other innovative people Ridley thinks are fascinating include Thomas Edison and Samuel Morse. Of course, many people already know about Edison and the light bulb. Morse's story, though, isn't as familiar to people.

Morse began his career as a painter. However, later in his life, Morse became interested in the telegraph. In fact, Morse began spending most of his time, making improvements to the existing telegraph technology.

Not only was Morse innovative, but he was also very persistent. In other words, Morse didn't give up when he encountered an obstacle. Indeed, Ridley has noticed that innovative people are also very persistent.

Although innovative people are persistent, it doesn't mean they never make mistakes. For example, look at Jeff Bezos, the founder of Amazon. He has made a lot of business mistakes. However, since Bezos was also able to make some good decisions, Amazon became a successful company.

Though Ridley writes books about innovation, he doesn't think of himself as being innovative. Of course, Altucher is shocked when Ridley says this. In fact, since Altucher admires his writing, he insists that Ridley's books are innovative.

Needless to say, I was impressed with this podcast episode. Although I haven't yet read any of Ridley's books, I enjoyed learning about them. Indeed, if you are someone who wants to become more innovative, you should listen to this interview.

The next podcast episode I want to share is about a famous novelist. In case you are curious, Ken Follett is the author Altucher interviews. If you have ever thought about writing a novel, then episode #804 will be perfect for you.

Although Follett has sold millions of books, he wasn't an overnight success. In fact, Follett wrote ten novels that flopped before he figured out what he was doing. Thankfully, though, Follett became a successful writer when he wrote *Eye of the Needle*.

I remember reading this book many years ago. To be honest, though, the only thing I remember about it is that I liked it. However, James Altucher has read many of Follet's books. Indeed, this is the reason Altucher is the right person to interview him.

The most recent novel Follet wrote is called *Never*. It's a lengthy novel, and Altucher enjoyed reading it. Of course, because Altucher loves Follett's novels, he also wants to learn about his writing secrets.

Since Follet has been writing books for fifty years, he was able to share a lot of writing tips with Altucher. If you listen carefully to this interview, you will also be able to learn from Follett. Although most of Follet's advice is brilliant, I don't agree with everything he says.

For example, Follett suggests reading a lot of books to prepare yourself to be a writer. This sounds like good advice, but I don't believe it's true. However, I do think that some reading is necessary when you're doing research.

Although I criticized one of Follett's writing tips, I still think he is an amazing author. So, if you want to be a writer, then please listen to this podcast episode. Now, though, it's time to move on to chapter four.

CHAPTER 4
ENTREPRENEURS ON FIRE

John Lee Dumas is the creator of the *Entrepreneurs on Fire* podcast. For those who don't know, this is a business-oriented show. Also, the podcast episodes on this podcast aren't very long. Indeed, I wish they *were* longer.

However, I do believe that when Dumas interviews entre-preneurs, his podcast is valuable to his listeners. Dumas refers to his listeners as Fire Nation. Although I don't con-sider myself part of Fire Nation, I have learned a lot from his podcast.

So, let's start out by learning about Dumas's interview with Greg McKeown. If you want to listen to this episode on Stitcher, it occurred on November 24, 2021. Of course, Dumas was happy to interview McKeown since he is a fa-mous author.

The book that made McKeown famous is called *Essential-ism*. Indeed, this book has helped many people decide what's important in their lives. This is great because some people have trouble setting priorities.

If you think you need help deciding on your priorities, then this would be a good book for you to read. More recently, though, McKeown has written a book called *Effortless*. Although his new book is similar to his old one, it makes sense to read both of them.

Thankfully, entrepreneurs can make more money if they take McKeown's ideas seriously. Not only can people make more money by learning his tactics, but they also won't get so worn out. Of course, making more money with less work is something that entrepreneurs want to learn about.

Naturally, John Lee Dumas was also interested in learning from Greg McKeown. To find out more about McKeown's ideas, I encourage you to listen to this interview. Also, his books are available at your local library.

Now, it's time to learn about *The Long Game*. Indeed, *The Long Game* is a book written by Dorie Clark. Not only is Clark an author, but she is also a professor. If you want to listen to this interview, it takes place on September 22, 2021.

When Dumas is interviewing Clark, it's obvious he has a great deal of respect for her. The reason Dumas is impressed with Clark is because she knows a lot about the business world. Fortunately, Clark is also someone I have known about for several years.

It's interesting that when Clark was growing up, she was very impatient. In fact, when her mother told her to be patient, she became even more impatient. Now that Clark is an adult, though, she has become a patient person.

This doesn't mean Clark doesn't work towards her goals. Instead, it means she has learned how to play the long game. So, what exactly is the long game? Clark believes the long game is realizing that sometimes it takes a while to accomplish your goals.

Although having patience is a simple idea, it's also something that is difficult for most people. Sadly, many people give up too quickly on their goals. Of course, Clark doesn't want you to give up. Indeed, since she is a kind person who wants to see you succeed.

Playing the long game, though, doesn't mean you will accomplish all your goals. In fact, even Clark has had goals that she failed to accomplish. However, by being patient, Clark has also accomplished some big things.

Something I like about Dorie Clark is that she has a cheerful and enthusiastic personality. To be honest, it's hard to believe that Clark is also a professor at Duke. If you want to learn about the business world, listen to this podcast episode.

Now it's time to learn about Google and a few other search engines. On August 18, 2021, John Lee Dumas interviewed Nick Loper. Although Loper is knowledgeable about many things, this interview is mostly about Google.

Right now, you're probably wondering, "What does Google have to do with becoming an entrepreneur?" Believe it or not, Google is more important than you might think. For example, if you write an article, you will want people to be able to find it on Google.

Of course, people won't be able to learn about your article if you aren't ranking high in the search results. In other words, if you want to sell your products and services, you need to figure out how Google works.

Google is the biggest search engine, but it isn't the only important one. Indeed, YouTube, Facebook, Amazon, and Pinterest, are also important search engines. So, try to also get good search results rankings on these other types of search engines.

Although figuring out Google's algorithms might not seem interesting, it's something you need to learn. As you can see, there is more to becoming an entrepreneur than you might have originally thought.

For a change of pace, let's learn more about James Altucher. As you probably remember, in the previous chapter we learned about *The James Altucher Show*. However, in this chapter, Altucher is a guest on the *Entrepreneurs on Fire* podcast.

This makes sense, since Altucher and Dumas are good friends. In case you're curious, this interview takes place on June 2, 2021. In this interview Altucher talks about a new book he has written.

Altucher's book is called *Skip The Line*. Sadly, when I first learned about the title of his book, I couldn't figure out what Altucher's book was about. However, *Skip The Line* is based on a simple idea.

Indeed, the basic idea of this book is that there is nothing preventing you from accomplishing your goals. This advice might seem strange, though, since the gatekeepers are always telling us we aren't good enough.

In fact, even people who aren't gatekeepers, will often try to discourage you from following your dreams. Although, some of these people think they are helping you, they really aren't. So, instead of allowing other people to destroy your dreams, believe in yourself.

The reason Altucher knows so much about outsmarting the gatekeepers is because he learned how to do it through personal experience. For example, there was a time when Altucher decided he would become a comedian.

Of course, breaking into comedy is a tough business. Altucher, though, was determined to become a successful comedian. So, he began to practice his comedy routine on the New York City subways.

Although it wasn't easy telling jokes to people on the subway, this was how Altucher perfected his comedy routine. Fortunately, you will probably never need to tell jokes on a subway. However, if you listen to this podcast interview you will learn how to Skip The Line.

Now let's learn about *The Money Tree*. For those who don't know, *The Money Tree* is a book Chris Guillebeau wrote.

Although Guillebeau is one of my favorite authors, this is a book I haven't yet read.

If you're interested in listening to Dumas interview Guillebeau, this podcast episode takes place on April 17, 2020. The first thing you will notice in this interview is that Dumas and Guillebeau are good friends. Indeed, both men have learned a lot from each other over the past several years.

Dumas, though, is really happy that Guillebeau wrote *The Money Tree*. What makes this book interesting is that it isn't your typical business book. Instead, Guillebeau tells a story about a young man named Jake.

This isn't a true story; it is a business parable. To make a long story short, Jake is a man who has a lot of financial problems. Sadly, not only is Jake struggling to pay his bills, but his girlfriend is thinking about leaving him.

This sounds like a lot of drama, but *The Money Tree* sounds like the kind of book I would want to read. Thankfully, since John Lee Dumas has read most of this book, he is the right person to be interviewing Chris Guillebeau.

Indeed, Dumas admits that when he first started reading *The Money Tree*, he didn't like the main character because he thought Jake was too whiny. However, when Jake starts becoming more responsible, Dumas discovers that he really likes the young man.

Dumas also liked the business lessons that can be learned by reading *The Money Tree*. Now, though, I want to introduce you to Seth Godin. Although, I have never met Godin, I feel like I already know him because I have read some of his books. I haven't read Godin's new book, which is called *The Practice*, but Dumas interviews Godin, on December 16, 2020.

For those who don't know, in the business world, Seth Godin is kind of a big deal. Indeed, if you go to your local library, you will find many of his books in the business section. However, I must warn you that Godin is a deep thinker.

In fact, I listened to this interview twice because there are so many important ideas in this episode. For example, Godin doesn't believe there is such a thing as writer's block. He does believe, though, that many people are afraid of writing poorly.

I agree with Godin on this point. Sadly, many people think writer's block is real. Indeed, I have had many people ask me, "How do you deal with writer's block?" Of course, they are disappointed when I tell them that writer's block doesn't exist.

Not only that, but many people who don't write, tell me that they are certain that writer's block exists. Then, when I don't agree with them, they look at me look at me like I'm a crazy nut. However, since Godin has written many books, he understands that writer's block isn't real.

For example, Godin asks Dumas, "How many podcasts have you recorded?" Dumas responds with a large number. Then Godin makes the point that there are people who have podcaster's block. In other words, someone who hasn't recorded a podcast episode might think they are not capable of doing it.

Another good point Godin makes is that we can learn how to have a good attitude. Sadly, someone with a bad attitude might think it's impossible to better themselves. Godin, though, believes that having a good attitude is a skill that can be learned.

Although I have barely scratched the surface of this interview, you can listen to the rest of it on Stitcher. While we are almost to the end of this chapter, we still have time to learn about John Jantsch.

On August 17, 2021, Dumas interviewed Jantsch. To be honest, I have known about Jantsch much longer than I have known about Dumas. Not only does Jantsch write books about marketing, but he also has his own podcast. In fact, I will be telling you about Jantsch's podcast in the next chapter.

Interestingly enough, this is the third time Jantsch has been a guest on *The Entrepreneurs on Fire* podcast. Since Jantsch is an expert in marketing, Dumas really admires him. Something else Dumas likes is that Jantsch explains important concepts in a simple way.

During this interview, Jantsch tells Dumas about his new marketing book. Not only does Jantsch write books and have his own podcast, but he also is a marketing strategist. In other words, Jantsch has clients who pay him for his expertise.

Unfortunately, though, many people don't know that they need Jantsch's help. Indeed, since most people don't know what a marketing strategist does, Jantsch looks for other words to describe his services.

Thankfully, Jantsch is an honest man who gives valuable advice to his clients. However, if you can't afford to hire Jantsch, you can still read his books and listen to his podcast even though you will still need to figure out some things for yourself.

Now it's time learn about the *Duct Tape Marketing* podcast. Are you ready to learn more about the business world?

CHAPTER 5
DUCT TAPE MARKETING

John Jantsch is the creator of the *Duct Tape Marketing* podcast. Since Jantsch has had many great guests on his show, I enjoy listening to his podcast. Right now, you're probably wondering, "Why is this podcast called *Duct Tape Marketing*?"

It's called *Duct Tape Marketing* because that is the title of one of Jantsch's books. The best way to learn about this podcast, though, is for me to tell you about some of the interviews. So, let's start by learning about business coaching.

Since Marc Mawhinney is a coaching expert, Jantsch is eager to interview him. Indeed, this interview takes place on February 16, 2022, and I recommend listening to it on Stitcher.

Many people would like to learn how to become a coach. However, when they see how hard it is to get clients, they become discouraged. For example, I want to become a book coach, but I haven't yet made any money from this business idea.

What Mawhinney is good at, though, is teaching coaches how to get clients. In other words, he is a coach for coaches. Also, Mawhinney has a podcast called *Natural Born Coaches*.

Needless to say, I encourage you to listen to his podcast. In fact, I'm so impressed with Mawhinney's podcast that I will be talking about it in the next chapter.

Now, though, it's time to learn how to Get Different. Indeed, *Get Different* is a book written by Mike Michalowicz. Not only is Michalowicz the author of *Get Different*, but he has also written several other business books.

Jantsch is happy to interview Michalowicz since the two men are friends. In case you're curious, this interview takes place on January 20, 2022. During this interview, you will learn how to attract clients by being a little bit different. Although you need to be different than your competitors, Michalowicz doesn't want you to take this too far.

For example, don't dress up like a clown, because clowns are creepy.

However, sometimes being different can help you establish your brand. Indeed, back in the old days, a company called Geek Squad caused a lot of problems for Michalowicz.

Back then, Michalowicz owned a computer company which was similar to Geek Squad. He was outsmarted by his competitor, though. The way Geek Squad outsmarted Michalowicz was to have their employees dress like geeks.

In other words, Geek Squad was successful because they were different. Although Michalowicz had to learn a tough lesson, he is now a more savvy businessman. So, learn from Michalowicz's mistakes by listening to this interview.

Have you ever wondered, "Why isn't there enough time in the day?" I know I sometimes feel this way. Thankfully, there is a fellow named Oliver Burkeman who spends a lot of time thinking about time. Although this might not sound like an interesting topic, it's actually more interesting than you might think.

Indeed, for those who are interested, John Jantsch interviews Burkeman on December 22, 2021. During this podcast episode, you will learn about Burkeman's new book, which is called *Four Thousand Weeks*. The reason his book is called this is because most people live about four thousand weeks.

Although realizing that life is short might frighten you, Burkeman doesn't want you to be scared. Instead, he wants you to understand that you need to set priorities for your life. Actually, though, you are already setting priorities for your life even if you don't realize it.

Unfortunately, sometimes we try to do too much. Indeed, Burkeman says that doing too much isn't good, because then you feel like you're on a treadmill. Of course, no rational person wants to feel like this.

So, how do you prevent yourself from doing too much? The answer is that you learn how to say no. Sometimes, it's hard to do this, though, when you want to please other people. However, when you try to please everyone, you will end up wearing yourself out.

It isn't always other people, though, who cause you to feel stressed. Sadly, sometimes we are the ones who set too many goals for ourselves. For some reason, we try to do more than we are capable of doing.

Please don't do this. You will only succeed in making yourself miserable. The bottom-line, though, is that you need to learn what to say yes to, and what to say no to. As you can see, Burkeman is a fellow who has a lot of wisdom.

It's time now to learn about fandom. For those who don't know, fandom is when you're a fan of something. For example, you might be a fan of a basketball team. Of course, when you're a fan of something, you will learn there are other people who love what you love.

David Meerman Scott actually wrote a book about Fandom. Of course, since Scott is a famous author, Jantsch was happy to interview him. This interview took place on January 7, 2020.

The title of Scott's new book is *Fanocracy*, and his daughter Reiko was his co-author. Although Reiko wasn't part of the interview, you can tell that Scott really loves his daughter. In fact, it's worth listening to this podcast episode just to learn about Reiko.

Something fascinating about David Meerman Scott is that he is a fan of the Grateful Dead. Not only is Scott a fan of this group, but he has attended many of their concerts. Although, being a fan of a rock group might not seem important, it helped Scott in the business world.

The reason that it helped him is because being a fan allowed him to meet another Grateful Dead fan named Brian Halligan. For those who don't know, Halligan is the co-founder of the HubSpot website. In fact, when Halligan discovered that Scott loved The Grateful Dead, he placed him on his advisory board.

Halligan and Scott are still good friends, and they have attended many Grateful Dead concerts together. Hopefully, you are beginning to realize that being a fan can help you in the business world.

Although, it's good to be a fan, it's even better when other people love your products and services. In other words, if you want to make a lot of money, you need to have fans. Of course, many people in the business world would love to have fans.

Unfortunately, most of these entrepreneurs don't understand how to turn their customers into fans. Thankfully, Scott will give you examples of how to do this. One example he mentions, is a car insurance company.

In case you don't know, most people hate buying car insurance. However, there is one car insurance company that has enthusiastic fans. This insurance company is called Hagerty. So, how does Hagerty do it?

How do they sell a product that nobody seems to want? The answer is that Hagerty builds a relationship with their customers. Indeed, they provide such great service that people are happy to buy whatever Hagerty is selling.

It sounds like Scott and his daughter have written an amazing book. So, if you want to learn more about *Fanocracy*, then please listen to this interview. Although, this isn't a lengthy interview, you will learn a lot from it.

Have you ever wondered, "Why do people create podcasts?" One of the reasons they people create podcasts is to make a lot of money. Unfortunately, not every podcaster is going to become wealthy.

There is a new podcaster, though, who I think will be very successful. If you're curious, his name is Guy Kawasaki. Not only is Kawasaki a new podcaster, but he is also a famous author.

When this interview took place, on January 29, 2020, Kawasaki had only recorded a few interviews for his own podcast. Now, though, his Remarkable People podcast has over 100 episodes. In fact, I'm so impressed with Kawasaki's podcast that I will be telling you about it in chapter seven.

During this interview, it's fun to see how enthusiastic Kawasaki is about podcasting. Although he is excited about his own podcast, he also enjoys listening to other peoples' podcasts. John Jantsch does a good job of interviewing Kawasaki, and it's obvious that the two men have respect for each other.

We learn something else in this podcast episode. We learn he is also a surfer. Indeed, I admire him for learning how to surf, even though he is certainly not a teenager. Since, Kawasaki lives in Hawaii, he can surf as much as he wants to.

The main takeaway from this interview, though, is that it's possible to make a lot of money with your own podcast. In fact, Kawasaki believes he can make more money with his podcast than he gets from writing books.

Since I'm starting a podcast, I was happy to learn that Kawasaki is also a podcaster. However, even if you're not interested in becoming a podcaster, I think you will still enjoy this interview.

Although, we have talked a lot about business in this chapter, I'm now going to tell you about mountain climbing. Sadly, though, what I know about climbing mountains is minimal. Indeed, it's been a while since I climbed even a small mountain.

Alison Levine, though, is a lady who has climbed many mountains. Interestingly enough, the first mountain Levine climbed was Mount Kilimanjaro. It wasn't an easy mountain to climb, but somehow, she did it.

Since Levine has had many exciting adventures, Jantsch was happy to interview her. For those interested, this interview takes place on September 4, 2020. Also, if you're not sure how to access this interview, I recommend listening to it on Stitcher.

After climbing Mount Kilimanjaro, Levine wanted to climb some more mountains. Although, it wasn't easy to climb them, she became very good at it. In fact, Levine even climbed to the top of Mount Everest.

Of course, climbing mountains is dangerous. Indeed, many people have died trying to climb Mount Everest. According to Levine, though, reaching the summit of Mount Everest isn't the most dangerous part of climbing the mountain.

Instead, she believes that returning from the summit is what's really dangerous because you are so exhausted at that point. In fact, some people die after climbing to the top of Mount Everest.

Even though Levine was a famous mountain climber, she also wanted to become a public speaker. Sadly, though, nobody wanted to give her a chance. But then somebody asked her, "Can you give a speech in Las Vegas?"

Of course, she agreed to speak in Las Vegas, and she caught the next flight there. Soon Levine was in Las Vegas. The only problem was she had to give a speech to 5,000 people. So, Levine stayed up all night preparing her speech.

Thankfully, when she gave her speech, everybody loved it. In fact, giving this speech opened up many speaking opportunities for Levine. In other words, when Levine accepted this speaking assignment, she made a good decision.

Although you might not be interested in becoming a public speaker, it doesn't mean her story is irrelevant. Indeed, the reason Levine tells this story is to encourage you to accomplish your own goals.

Since, Levine is an enthusiastic person, you will soon find yourself wondering, "What would it be like to climb Mount

Everest?" Of course, now that I'm older, this is nothing more than a daydream for me. However, when I was a young man, this is something I would have actually done.

Please don't tell my mother about my adventurous side, though. She would not be pleased. I don't think my girlfriend would like it either.

As you have seen from this chapter, the *Duct Tape Marketing* podcast is an amazing resource. I've learned a lot from this fantastic show. Now, though, it's time to learn about the *Natural Born Coaches* podcast.

CHAPTER 6
NATURAL BORN COACHES

Marc Mawhinney is the person who started the *Natural Born Coaches* podcast. Since Mawhinney teaches people how to become coaches in the business world, he is someone I really admire. Although you might not be interested in becoming a coach, you may change your mind after reading this chapter.

So, let's begin by learning how to become a guest on podcasts. For those of you who have never thought about being a podcast guest, this might seem like an unusual topic. However, being a guest on podcasts can help you sell your products and services.

A fellow named Jeremy Slate knows a lot about this topic. Mawhinney interviews Slate in episode #732, and I'm going to suggest that you listen to this interview on Stitcher.

The first thing Slate recommends is to not start off by expecting to be on the most popular podcasts. Instead, you should begin by being a guest on some of the smaller podcasts. In other words, don't get too big for your britches.

Something else Slate suggests is that you need to approach podcasters in the right way. For example, don't tell a podcaster you love their show if you haven't actually listened to it. Also, make sure you know a podcaster's name before you try to get on their show.

Believe it or not, Slate once had someone call him by his middle name. Not only was this irritating, but that person never became a guest on his podcast. The bottom-line, you need to have some common sense if you want to get booked on podcasts.

Now, for a change of pace, let's learn about productivity. In episode #654, Mawhinney interviews Tommy Baker about this topic. Although I'm already a productive person, for some reason I'm still fascinated with learning more about productivity.

According to Baker, the first step to becoming productive is to figure out your priorities. For example, one of my priorities was to write the book you are currently reading. Since you're now reading this book, this means I was successful in accomplishing an important goal.

The problem is that many people don't know what their priorities are. So, instead of doing something that's important, they end up wasting their time. To be honest, I used to be one of those people. But thankfully I eventually learned how to set priorities for myself.

However, Baker says it isn't enough to just set priorities. Indeed, after you set your priorities, you need to create boundaries. In other words, don't stop working on an important project in order to have coffee with someone.

For a people person, this might sound like harsh advice. In fact, you might say to yourself, "What's wrong with socializing?" Of course, nothing is wrong with socializing after you have finished your work.

Although this might be advice you didn't want to hear, Baker is right. I'm not saying that creating boundaries is easy, but it is necessary. To be honest, when you create boundaries, some people will think you're a real jackass.

The good news, though, is that the same people who are mad at you, will also admire you for being productive. Although the last few paragraphs are my own thoughts, I don't think I'm wrong. However, to get the full impact from this interview with Tommy Baker, I suggest listening to it on Stitcher.

Many people want to write a book. In fact, you might be one of them. Writing a book is the easy part. By now you're probably wondering, "What is the hard part of writing a book?"

The difficult part of writing a book is figuring out how to market it. Although you might think marketing a book is simple, it really isn't. Thankfully, though, Emee Estacio is an expert at selling books on Amazon.

Indeed, Marc Mawhinney was so impressed with Estacio that he interviews her in episode #694. The first thing you will learn about Estacio is that she is very smart. Of course, there are many smart people in the world, but most of them don't have a PhD in psychology.

Not only does Estacio write and sell books on Amazon, but she also teaches other people how to do it. Estacio says that the first thing to understand about Amazon is that it's a giant search engine. In other words, Amazon is similar to Google.

Although, realizing that Amazon is a search engine is fascinating, you're probably wondering, "What does this have to do with me?" If you're planning on selling your book on Amazon's website, this is something you need to know.

Something else you need to know is how to turn your book into an Amazon bestseller. If this sounds like an impossible task, don't panic. There are 10,000 book categories on Amazon. In other words, your book can become an Amazon bestseller in an obscure category.

The bottom-line, though, is that Estacio can teach you how to market your book. If this is something that interests you, I encourage you to listen to this podcast episode. Now, though, it's time to learn about networking.

In the business world, you can become wealthy if you know how to network. Most people aren't very good at it, and to be honest, I know very little about it myself. Thankfully, Michael Whitehouse is an expert on this topic.

In episode #749, Marc Mawhinney interviews Whitehouse. During this interview, Whitehouse says he wasn't always an expert on networking. However, gradually he began to figure out how to build business relationships.

Indeed, everything was going great for Whitehouse before the pandemic. After the pandemic hit, though, he had to learn how to use the Internet for his networking. In other words, Whitehouse had to figure out a different way to connect with people.

It's interesting that Whitehouse became even more successful during the pandemic. Of course, if you're like me, you're probably wondering, "How did he do this?" The answer is that the Internet allowed Whitehouse to connect with people from all over the world instead of just those who live close to him. Now Whitehouse can also connect with people in other countries.

Hopefully you're beginning to realize that networking is important. Whitehouse wants you to understand that you can also be a networker. In fact, he even wrote a book on this subject that is titled: *The Guy Who knows A Guy*. Since networking is something I want to learn about, I have started reading Whitehouse's book. Thankfully, it's a short book I know I will be able to finish.

Something I've already learned from Whitehouse's book is that resumes don't work. At least they don't work very well. In other words, if you are serious about finding a job, you need to learn about networking.

As you can see, Michael Whitehouse is truly an expert at building business relationships. Although networking might not be a glamorous topic, I still hope you listen to this interview.

Let's talk about procrastination. Back in the old days, I used to be an expert at procrastinating. Although now I have learned how to stop procrastinating, many people can't seem to get started with their projects.

Fortunately, there is a lady who teaches people that they don't need to procrastinate. This lady's name is Nina Cooke, and Marc Mawhinney interviews her in episode #703.

As you listen to this episode, you will discover that Cooke teaches business owners how to stop procrastinating. Sometimes her business clients don't even know they're procrastinating.

Since, Cooke is a good coach, many of her clients become more productive. Thankfully, though, you can learn some of Cooke's secrets, even if you're not one of her clients. For example, sometimes there is a little voice inside your head that sabotages you.

Some people call this voice the ego. Sadly, your ego can be a real nuisance. Indeed, instead of helping you accomplish things, your ego works against you. Although, your ego seems powerful, that's only because you always let it have its way.

At first, it will be difficult to confront the little voice inside your head. However, gradually you will learn that you don't need to allow your ego to control your life. Then, when your ego isn't controlling your life, you won't procrastinate as much.

Also, when you stop procrastinating, you will be able to make a lot more money. Of course, there is much more to this interview than I have shared with you, so I encourage you to listen to this podcast episode.

Now it's time to learn about relationship-building. To avoid any confusion, I'm not talking about romantic relationships. Instead, I will be telling you about a man who knows how to build business relationships.

Indeed, Mawhinney interviews Steve Chandler in episode #686. The first thing I noticed while listening to Chandler is that he has a lot of wisdom. As I explain some of Chandler's business ideas, I think you will also be impressed with him.

To begin with, Chandler isn't a high-pressure salesman. In fact, he even discourages his students from using high-pressure sales tactics. When Chandler first became a coach, he didn't know to build business relationships.

This wasn't good because it made it difficult for him to get clients. However, after a couple of years of doing things the wrong way, Chandler finally figured out how to run his coaching business.

In fact, it was Chandler's coach who taught him the right way to talk to potential clients. For example, his coach taught him that he didn't have to feel bad if someone didn't want to become his client.

Instead of feeling bad, Chandler simply put this person on his not-yet list.

The nice thing about this approach to selling is that he didn't make other people feel uncomfortable. In fact, his potential clients quickly realized that he wasn't just trying to make money from them.

Later on, though, Chandler would contact the people on his not-yet list to see how they were doing. Since Chandler was a friendly person, they didn't mind talking to him. Some of the people on his not-yet list eventually became his coaching clients.

After he learned this method for getting clients, Chandler began teaching other people how to do the same thing. Also, he started writing books. In fact, Chandler has written over thirty books.

Since Chandler is an older gentleman, he has had the opportunity to help many people during his coaching career. So, if learning how to get clients sounds interesting to you, then I suggest listening to this podcast episode.

While this chapter is nearing the end, I still have time to tell you about an Italian fellow named Simone Vincenzi. For those who want to listen to this interview, it's episode #683.

When Vincenzi was a young man, he wasn't interested in attending college. Something he did like, though, was eating Italian food. Since Italian food is so delicious, this is something I can relate to.

But after working as a waiter in an Italian restaurant, Vincenzi decided to become a coach. Although he wanted to get clients, everybody thought Vincenzi was too young. He was only 22 years old, but Vincenzi had no intention of giving up on his dream.

To make a long story short, some of the big shots in the business world liked the things Vincenzi was saying. In fact, these businessmen asked him to speak in front of large audiences.

In other words, Vincenzi had an important message to share with the world, and eventually his persistence paid off. Needless to say, I'm also impressed with Vincenzi, and I will be telling you more about him in chapter nine. However, now let's learn about *Remarkable People.*

CHAPTER 7
REMARKABLE PEOPLE

Guy Kawasaki started the *Remarkable People* podcast. Although, he has only been podcasting for two years, Kawasaki has already created quite a few podcast episodes. Indeed, he interviews a new guest every week.

These aren't any short interviews, though, so you will need to set aside nearly an hour to listen to an episode. The first interview that I want to tell you about, focuses on the topic of persuasion. This podcast episode with Robert Cialdini took place on January 15, 2020, and I recommend listening to it on Stitcher.

For those who don't know, Cialdini is kind of a big deal in the business world. However, when he was a young man, Cialdini was mostly interested in baseball. In fact, Cialdini almost became a Minor League Baseball player.

Instead, Cialdini decided to go to college. Thankfully, this turned out to be a good decision, since he wasn't talented enough to become a Major League player. In college, though, Cialdini was a great student.

Not only was he a great student, but he also became a professor. Although Guy Kawasaki was never one of Cialdini's college students, he still admires him. Indeed, many people in the business world have learned a lot from reading Cialdini's books.

Although he is a master of persuasion, Cialdini doesn't want people to use his ideas in the wrong way. For example, Cialdini recently visited an electronics store. While he was there, Cialdini saw a big screen TV he wanted to buy.

Just at that moment, a salesman noticed he was interested in the television. Quickly, the salesman approached Cialdini and told him that was the last TV of this type in the store. Of course, he didn't want to miss out on a great deal, so Cialdini bought the big screen TV.

When he got home Cialdini began to wonder if the salesman was honest with him. Since there was only one way to find out, Cialdini returned to the electronics store the next day and discovered the salesman had told him the truth.

Cialdini knew the salesman had been honest because there was an empty spot where his TV had been. This made Cialdini happy that the salesman had used a persuasion technique in the right way. In fact, he was so pleased with the salesman that Cialdini wrote a good review for him.

If you want to learn about Cialdini's persuasion techniques, listen to this podcast episode. Now I want to tell you about a fellow named Gary Vaynerchuk. Although Vaynerchuk is an expert in marketing, he also curses a lot.

However, Vaynerchuk tries not to swear during his interview with Kawasaki. To be honest, I prefer listening to Vaynerchuk when he isn't continually cursing.

Also, even though Kawasaki and Vaynerchuk are friends, Kawasaki tells Vaynerchuk that he swears too much. Now that I have told you this, you will probably want to listen to this podcast episode. If this is the case, this interview took place on April 1, 2020.

One of the first things you will notice about Vaynerchuk is that he is a clever businessman. For example, back in the old days, he invested in Facebook. Needless to say, Vaynerchuk made a lot of money on this investment.

Since Vaynerchuk is a savvy investor, Kawasaki asks his friend for investment advice. He is surprised, though, when Vaynerchuk tells him that he should invest in sports cards. That's confusing to Kawasaki because he had never thought about investing in basketball and baseball cards.

The real value of listening to Vaynerchuk, though, is that he can teach you how to sell your products and services. Although, you can get some marketing ideas from Vaynerchuk in this interview, I also suggest reading his books.

Vaynerchuk's newest book is *Twelve And A Half*. Thankfully, I was able to buy this book at a library book sale for only a dollar. Although I have just started reading it, I can tell that it's an informative book.

Another good way to learn from Vaynerchuk is to listen to his podcast. Something to be aware of, though, is that he doesn't always have guests on his show. In other words, during many of his podcast episodes Vaynerchuk gives advice directly to you.

Since Vaynerchuk has a lot of wisdom, many people want to learn from him. Indeed, this is the reason Guy Kawasaki had Gary Vaynerchuk as a guest on his *Remarkable People* podcast.

Now let's learn about Melanie Perkins. For those who don't know, Perkins is Kawasaki's boss. In fact, not only is she his boss, but Perkins is also a powerful Australian businesswoman.

Although things are going good for her now, she had to struggle in the beginning. Before I go any further, though, let me mention that this podcast episode takes place on August 5, 2020. Now, let's return to Perkins story.

Back in 2007, Perkins and her boyfriend, Cliff Obrecht, started a company called Fusion Books. The purpose of the company was to provide the technology which would make it easier for students to design their yearbooks.

Later on, though, Perkins and Obrecht started a company called Canva. For those who don't know, Canva is basically a simplified version of Photoshop that is much easier to use.

Sadly, Perkins initially had trouble finding anyone who wanted to invest in her company. However, although it took a while, eventually Perkins was able to raise the money she needed for her company.

Of course, since she is a savvy businesswoman, Perkins only hired the best people to work at Canva. For example, she hired Guy Kawasaki. Now, though, Canva is a company that's worth billions of dollars.

Since Kawasaki loves working at Canva, you can tell that he enjoyed interviewing his boss. Indeed, Kawasaki believes that Canva is one of the best companies he has worked for. Also, for those who are curious, Perkins and her boyfriend finally got married.

The main takeaway from this interview is that you need to be persistent if you want to be successful. Although it would have been easy for Perkins to give up, she kept working on her goals.

For a change of pace, let's learn about Tim Ferriss. If his name sounds familiar, it's because he is the person who wrote *The Four-Hour Workweek*. Before listening to this podcast episode, though, be aware that Ferriss swears a lot.

Not only is Ferriss a famous author, but he is also a successful podcaster. In fact, Ferris has one of the most popular podcasts on the planet. As you can see, Ferriss is a remarkable person, and Kawasaki is happy to interview him. If you want to listen to this podcast episode, it took place on September 30, 2020.

Although things are going good for Ferriss now, this wasn't always the case. Indeed, there was a time when he wanted to kill himself. Thankfully, though, Ferriss decided not to do that. To make a long story short, Ferriss has learned new ways of dealing with his depression.

Of course, topics such as suicide and depression aren't easy to talk about. Fortunately, though, Ferriss is willing to share the story of his struggle with severe depression. Although you might not be dealing with depression, you probably know someone who is.

Ferriss also talks about how he got started with his writing. To be honest, he really didn't want to write a book. However, when Ferriss told his friends that he was thinking about writing one, they encouraged him to do it.

Writing a book turned out to be a good decision for Ferris. Indeed, *The Four-Hour Workweek* became a New York Times Best Seller. Not only did Ferris write *The Four-Hour Workweek*, but he has also written several other books.

Although Ferriss believes that his books are important, he also enjoys podcasting. If you are interested in listening to his podcast, it's called *The Tim Ferris Show*. Since Ferriss has amazing guests on his podcast, I know you will like listening to it.

If what I have told you about Ferris sounds interesting, then listen to the interview. But now I want to tell you about someone who is an amazing teacher. His name is Sal Khan, and he is the person who created Khan Academy.

Even though Khan never received a teaching certificate; many people enjoy learning from him. Indeed, the first person Khan helped was his cousin. The reason he wanted to help Nadia was because she was struggling with math.

Before we continue with Khan's story, though, this interview took place on October 7, 2020. Although Nadia didn't think she could improve her math skills, it turned out she was wrong. In fact, Khan's cousin improved so much that she began studying mathematics with the advanced students in her school.

Of course, word quickly spread about the success Nadia had achieved in math. So, before he knew it, Khan was tutoring many of his cousins. Also, Khan began creating online videos of the content he was teaching.

Although it surprised him, Khan discovered that his cousins preferred learning from him on YouTube. Eventually, Khan created Khan Academy. This was great, because then the whole world was able to learn from Khan.

Speaking from personal experience, I can tell you that Khan's courses are top-notch. In fact, I have watched many of his history videos. To be more specific, Khan's history videos have given me an entirely new perspective on World War I.

Something Khan doesn't mention in his interview, though, is that you also get points and earn badges on Khan Academy. Although, this might seem childish, it does make the learning experience more enjoyable. Also, you need to be aware that many of the courses are designed for young children. Needless to say, I really admire Sal Khan. Indeed, he has helped many people by creating Khan Academy.

Now let's talk about a lady named Julia Cameron. For those who don't know, Cameron became famous when she wrote *The Artist's Way*. In fact, Cameron has sold five million copies of her book. If this sounds like Cameron has sold a ton of books, it's because she has.

Before we continue further, though, Kawasaki interviewed Cameron on January 13, 2021. Interestingly enough, not only has Cameron written *The Artist's Way*, she has also written many other books. Although Cameron is already a famous author, sometimes she doesn't have enough self-confidence.

She says there is a voice inside her head that tries to prevent her from accomplishing anything important. Since Cameron must deal with this critical voice on a regular basis, she decided to name him Nigel.

Although Nigel can be quite bossy, sometimes Cameron must let him know she is in charge. Indeed, if Cameron didn't put Nigel in his place, she would never have the opportunity to be creative.

To be honest, I think we all have our own inner critic, but thankfully, not everyone is going to name it Nigel. However, no matter what you name your inner critic, you still have the potential to be a creative and productive person.

Another interesting thing about Cameron is her method of writing. Believe it or not, she writes the first draft of her book in longhand. Although that isn't how I write my books, I admire Cameron for using a writing method that works for her.

Indeed, too many people never write a book because they spend too much time worrying about technology. So, instead of worrying about word processing software, write your book with a crayon if that's what it takes.

Now it's time to move on to chapter eight. Are you ready to start learning about Jonathan Fields and his amazing podcast?

CHAPTER 8
GOOD LIFE PROJECT

The Good Life Project is a podcast created by Jonathan Fields. Although I have only known about Fields for a short time, I'm impressed with his show. Of course, what makes his podcast interesting, are the guests he interviews.

The best way for you to learn about this show is for me to tell you about some of the episodes. On January 23, 2020, Fields interviewed Bishop Michael Curry. Since Curry is an important religious leader, I was especially interested in listening to this interview.

Although you might not be familiar with Curry's name, he is the Bishop who gave the sermon at the royal wedding. To be honest, I don't really care about Prince Harry or Meghan Markle. However, the royal wedding was an event that fascinated many people.

Not only did Michael Curry give an important sermon in England, but he is also a Bishop in the Episcopal Church. In fact, Curry is in charge of the Episcopal Church in the United States. Interestingly enough, Curry is also the first African American to hold this position.

Another important thing to know about Bishop Curry is that he cares about social justice issues. If you're not sure what this means, just think about Martin Luther King Jr. and how he helped the less fortunate.

Helping other people, though, isn't always easy. Indeed, King was arrested twenty-nine times, even though he was doing the right thing. According to Curry, the best way to help others is when your heart is filled with love.

Sadly, this can be difficult when you think about the people who have treated you badly. However, if your heart is filled with revenge, you won't be able to help others. So, do what the Good Book says and learn how to love other people.

As you can see, Bishop Curry is a very spiritual man. Now though, I want to introduce you to a famous author named Elizabeth Gilbert. She wrote *Eat, Pray, Love.* Not only has Gilbert written this book, but she has also written other books.

If this sounds like an interesting interview to you, it took place on November 1, 2020. Let me begin, though, by admitting that I haven't read any of Gilbert's books. After listening to this podcast episode, though, I'm able to understand why many people enjoy her writing.

Jonathan Fields' interview with Gilbert begins with her telling him about the death of her girlfriend. Sadly, Gilbert didn't realize she loved Rayya until her girlfriend got cancer. Indeed, Gilbert was so worried about her girlfriend that she stopped writing.

Rayya meant everything to Gilbert, and it broke her heart when her girlfriend died. After Rayya's death, though, Gilbert was able to start writing again. In fact, she began writing a novel about what life was like in New York City back in the 1940s.

For those who want to read this book, it's called *City of Girls*. I think Jonathan Fields must be a speed reader, though, because he has already read it. I also plan on reading this novel, but I want to read some of Gilbert's other books first.

Needless to say, I enjoyed listening to Elizabeth Gilbert, and I encourage you to listen to this podcast episode. Now, for a change of pace, let's learn about Bruce Feiler. Of course, the most important thing about Feiler, is that he was born in 1964.

The reason this is important is because that's the same year I was born. What's really interesting about Feiler, though, is the books he writes. For example, Feiler wrote a book that's called *Walking the Bible*. Before we go any further, this interview took place on September 9, 2020.

When Feiler wrote his book about the Bible, he actually ended up walking ten thousand miles. Although, it wasn't easy to walk through the deserts in the Middle East, he did it anyway. In other words, when Feiler called his book *Walking the Bible*, he wasn't joking.

I have to admit that I admire Feiler for going on an adventure like that. Sadly, though, Feiler has had challenges in his life. Indeed, Feiler was frightened when he discovered he had cancer in his leg.

What worried Feiler the most, though, was that his twin daughters would grow up without a father. Thankfully, Feiler didn't die, so he still gets to spend time with his family. Also, after surviving cancer, Feiler continued writing books.

Feiler's most recent book, though, is about the transitions we experience in our lives. Although usually we don't want our lives to change, unexpected things happen to us. For example, Feiler's father got Parkinson's disease.

Sadly, not only did his father get this terrible disease, but he also wanted to kill himself. Of course, this was upsetting to Feiler, and he didn't know how to help his father. Then Feiler decided to ask his dad to tell him stories about his life.

Thankfully, when his dad started remembering all the good things that had happened to him, he started feeling better. This didn't mean that the Parkinson's disease went away, but now his father had a better attitude.

After listening to this interview, I did some research and learned that Feiler's father recently died. Along with that I discovered his father's death hit Feiler much harder than he thought it would.

As you can see, Bruce Feiler is a deep thinker who really loves his family. Now, though, I want to tell you about another deep thinker named Dan Pink. Fields interviews him on January 30, 2022.

Regret is the topic they discuss. Ordinarily, I wouldn't listen to this type of interview, but I did anyway. Now that I have learned about regret, I'm glad I listened to this podcast episode.

The first thing to understand about regret is that you shouldn't be afraid of this emotion. Although it's easy to say, "I have no regrets", this statement isn't actually true. Indeed, if we are being honest with ourselves, we will realize we have many regrets.

This doesn't mean we need to spend all our time feeling bad about the mistakes we have made. Instead, Pink believes we should learn from the mistakes we make. Pink admits, though, that sometimes he doesn't deal with his regrets in the right way.

In fact, the problem Pink has, is that he is too tough on himself. He suggests that when you learn from your mistakes, you should show some compassion toward yourself. Although you want to hold yourself to high standards, nobody is perfect.

The reason Pink knows so much about regret is because he has done a lot of research on this topic. Indeed, some of Pink's research was asking people about their regrets. What surprised Pink, though, was that many people wanted to talk to him about this personal topic.

Some of the people Pink spoke with were still regretting things they had done a long time ago. For example, some people felt bad about bullying another person. Although their bad behavior might have happened forty years ago, they still felt awful about what they had done.

For some reason, these people felt much better when they told Pink about their regrets. Of course, bullying other people, isn't the only type of regret people have. Indeed, another regret that some people have is that they didn't ask someone out on a date.

Fear of rejection was probably the reason they didn't ask the person on a date. Some people, though, now wish that they hadn't been scared of rejection. In fact, even if that special person had ended up telling them no, they still regret not asking them.

After interviewing many people about their regrets, Dan Pink wrote a book about this topic. Although I haven't yet read Pink's book, it sounds like a good one. Before, you read his book, though, I suggest listening to this podcast episode.

Now it's time to learn about the different ways we delude ourselves. In other words, many of us believe things that aren't true. For example, everyone thinks they're a good driver. Unfortunately, this isn't always true.

In fact, some people who believe they are good drivers, are actually terrible drivers. Since it's very easy to delude ourselves Fields wanted Julia Galef to be a guest on his podcast. If this sounds interesting to you, this interview took place on August 22, 2021.

One of the first things you will learn about Galef in this interview is that she has written a book called *The Scout Mindset.* Since this title is confusing, Galef explains what her book is about.

First, she says there are two types of mindsets. The first type is the soldier mindset. Sadly, though, you won't become the person you want to be if you have this type of mindset. Of course, having a soldier mindset doesn't mean that you served in the military.

Instead, having this type of mindset means you always have to be right. The only problem with this type of thinking is that you aren't always right. So, this is why it's better to have a scout mindset.

A scout mindset is the opposite of a soldier mindset. When you have a scout mindset, you are a person who is curious. Although, it's easy to assume that you have all the answers, the truth is, you don't. So do your best to observe the world with a scout mindset.

I enjoyed listening to this interview with Galef because she likes to explore new ideas. However, if you want a deeper understanding of the scout mindset, you will need to listen to this interview.

Unfortunately, there is only time for me to tell you about one more podcast interview in this chapter. So, let's learn about Anne Lamott in an interview that took place on April 7, 2020.

Although Lamott now has a good life, when she was younger, she had quite a few problems. Sadly, one of her biggest problems was that she was an alcoholic. In fact, Lamott drank so much she would blackout.

To be honest, Lamott enjoyed drinking. What she didn't like, though, was waking up with a hangover. Of course, this wasn't the kind of life Lamott wanted to have, so she started attending church.

Since she hadn't stopped drinking, Lamott smelled bad when she went to church. Thankfully, though, the people at church didn't judge her. Instead, they only wanted the best for Lamott. Eventually she was able to stop drinking.

Even before Lamott stopped drinking she had written four books. Since writing books was important to Lamott, she continued writing them after she became sober. Lamott also discovered she enjoyed being a Christian.

Believing in Jesus was something new for her, though, since she was raised in an atheist home. Interestingly enough, not only did Lamott become a Christian, but she also became a Sunday school teacher.

Indeed, Lamott loves teaching the children at the small church she attends. Lamott learned, though, that part of being a good teacher is also being a good listener. So, she does her best to listen to her students.

What most people know about Lamott, though, is that she is a famous author. Although, I haven't yet read any of her books, I'm planning on reading *Bird By Bird*. For those who don't know, *Bird By Bird* is a book that teaches beginning writers how to become better writers.

As you can see, Anne Lamott has led a fascinating life. Althhough, she had many challenges when she was younger, Lamott became someone who many people admire. However, to get the full impact from this podcast episode, you will need to listen to the entire interview.

CHAPTER 9
EXPERT TO AUTHORITY

The *Expert To Authority* podcast was started by Simone Vincenzi. To be honest, I didn't know anything about Vincenzi until I wrote the sixth chapter of this book. Now that I have learned about Vincenzi, I have discovered he has a lot of wisdom.

Something else I discovered, is that I love Vincenzi's podcast. Indeed, when I listen to Vincenzi interview his guests, it's obvious that he enjoys talking to people. But he is also a good listener.

Vincenzi's podcast is focused on business topics. In episode #324, Vincenzi interviews Rachel Pedersen, a social media expert who became fascinated with the subject when she was quite young. Now she is a mother with children of her own.

Although Pedersen has had good experiences with social media, she realizes that social media also has a negative side. For example, some people on the Internet have said terrible things to her.

Of course, not everyone on the Internet is rude. In fact, most people you meet on social media websites are quite nice. So, focus on the positive feedback you receive instead of worrying about the haters.

The social media websites Pedersen likes the best are Tik-Tok and YouTube. Although many people in business are skeptical of TikTok, Pedersen has had great success with this social media platform.

An interesting fact about Pedersen is that she married her husband thirteen days after she met him. Of course, Pedersen's family and friends were worried about her, since this seemed like a bad decision. Thankfully though, Pedersen knew what she was doing, and she is still happily married.

Although, this is a great story, the main takeaway is that you need to learn more about social media. To be honest, I know that I need to learn more about this topic. Fortunately, if you listen to this podcast episode, you will get some great advice.

Now, though, it's time to learn about podcasting. Indeed, in episode #327, Vincenzi interviews Matt Nappo about this subject. Although I had never heard about Nappo before, I believe he has many good ideas.

Something important to Nappo, is that he thinks we should be careful with the words we use. He thinks many people give you their personal opinion when actually they are just repeating something they heard from someone else. I first observed this when I was in elementary school, so I agree with Nappo.

In other words, many people think their ideas are original, when they aren't. Sadly, many people are lazy, so they're not going to make the effort to think their own thoughts. Although, you can't control what other people do, make sure that you're not this type of person.

What I find really interesting about Nappo is that he is a podcaster. In fact, Nappo has recorded hundreds of episodes on his *MinddogTV* podcast. Of course, after I learned about Nappo's podcast, I had to listen to some of the episodes.

To make a long story short, I was very impressed with Nappo's podcast. Indeed, I was so impressed with it that I will be talking about it in the next chapter.

Now, though, it's time to learn about virtual assistants. In case you don't know, a virtual assistant is someone you hire on the Internet to help you with your work. Although you may not have ever thought about hiring a virtual assistant, now is a good time to start thinking about it.

Nathan Hirsch is an expert on outsourcing. Indeed, when you listen to Hirsch in episode #331, you will begin to understand how a virtual assistant can help you.

In fact, you might discover that you need several virtual assistants. However, before you start hiring people, there are a few things you need to know. For example, your virtual assistants aren't your slaves.

In other words, you need to treat your workers with respect. So, instead of thinking that you're a big shot, treat others the way you want to be treated. This advice should be common sense, but sadly, some entrepreneurs still have a lot to learn.

Something else to be aware of is that your virtual assistants probably aren't just working for you. Indeed, this is especially true if you hire part-time workers. Sometimes, though, you might want a virtual assistant to work exclusively for you.

If this is the case, then Hirsch suggests mentioning this to your workers. He has done this himself. In fact, Hirsch shares a story about asking one of his workers to work exclusively for him.

During their conversation, Hirsch discovered that his virtual assistant wanted a $1.50 per hour pay raise. Of course, since this person was an amazing worker, he didn't mind paying the extra money.

As you can see, Hirsch is very knowledgeable about outsourcing. So, if you're interested in learning more about this important topic, I encourage you to listen to this podcast episode.

Now, though, it's time to learn how to get paid what you're worth. In other words, if you're an entrepreneur, you're probably not charging your clients enough money for your services.

However, even if you aren't an entrepreneur, I still think it's important to learn that your time is valuable. Indeed, this is why I'm happy that Loren Fogelman was a guest on Vincenzi's podcast. For those who are interested, this interview is episode #357.

Before Fogelman became an expert in teaching people how to charge more money, she was a sports psychologist. This was interesting work, and many of Fogelman's clients were golfers. Although Fogelman enjoyed being a sports psychologist, she also likes her new job.

The first thing Fogelman suggests is that you shouldn't be paid by the hour. Even though this is what most people are used to, she thinks it's a bad idea. Instead, Fogelman recommends offering your clients a package deal.

However, even if you decide to stick with an hourly rate, don't be afraid to ask your clients for more money. Sometimes this isn't easy to do, though, because you think you will lose your clients.

Although it's true that you may lose some, that's alright, because these are the clients who never valued your expertise. So, to make a long story short, these people aren't your ideal clients.

Of course, it takes courage to ask for more money. So, it is important that you believe in yourself. By now, you're probably thinking, "I didn't know there was so much psychology involved with making more money."

The good news is that Fogelman knows a lot about this topic since she was a sports psychologist. So, if you are interested in learning how to get paid what you're worth, please listen to this interview.

Now, for a change of pace, let's learn about the martial arts in episode #357. When John Terry was a boy, he was bullied by the other kids in school. Since his father was worried about him, he signed his son up for Karate lessons.

After Terry began learning how to defend himself, nobody wanted to pick on him. But just knowing how to defend himself wasn't enough for Terry. In fact, Terry became a black belt in several different types of martial arts.

Although Terry was fascinated with the martial arts at a young age, he was also interested in making money. Then one day an influential man told Terry he should write a book. This advice was confusing to Terry since he was only 23 years old.

To be honest, Terry thought he was too young to write a book. Indeed, he didn't think anyone would be interested in any of his ideas. Someone believed in Terry, though, and told him to write the book.

In case you're wondering who believed in Terry, it was his mother. In fact, she told him that if only one person was influenced by his book, then he should write it. So, Terry did what his mother told him to do, and he wrote a book. Fortunately, though, to Terry's surprise, many people enjoyed reading his book.

Then, after Terry wrote his first book, he decided to continue writing books. In addition to writing books, Terry also became a talented public speaker. Indeed, when I was listening to this interview, I could picture Terry speaking before a large audience.

Terry has now become an important person in the business world. So, if you want to learn from someone who is very articulate, then I encourage you to listen to this interview.

Now let's learn about sales. Although sales might not seem like an interesting topic, you will become fascinated with it when you're not making any money. Thankfully, though, Eddie Sand is an expert in sales, and Vincenzi interviews him in episode #374.

However, when Sand first got started in sales, he had no idea what he was doing. The reason he didn't know anything about sales was because his only work experience was in the military.

Gradually, though, Sand became a better salesman. Of course, it made Sand happy to see the progress he was making as a salesman.

A by-product of becoming a better salesman was that Sand no longer felt awkward when he was talking to other people. Indeed, why should he feel awkward when he was only sharing valuable information?

Interestingly enough, Sand had no desire to pressure someone into buying something they didn't want. Instead, Sand only wanted to work with clients who were ready to buy what he was selling. In other words, Sand spent his time looking for ideal clients.

If you think about it, this makes sense. Although most salesmen try to sell to everyone, this is actually a bad idea. In fact, when you do this, you will end up with clients who don't appreciate your products and services. So, instead of doing things the hard way, I encourage you to learn about Sand's sales methods.

As you can see, there is a lot more to sales than you probably thought there was. However, if you want to learn more about this important topic, then you should listen to this podcast episode.

Finally in this chapter, let's learn about leadership from Amy Riley. Vincenzi interviews Riley about this topic in episode #370.

Although a lot goes into becoming a leader, it's important to think about your leadership legacy. To be honest, when Riley first mentioned this term, I was a bit confused. In fact, I didn't even know that leadership legacy was a thing.

However, your leadership legacy is how other people will remember you. If you're a young person, you're probably thinking, "I'm too young to be worrying about my leadership legacy." According to many business experts, though, you're never too young to start thinking about this topic.

Indeed, you can also create a leadership legacy statement for yourself. Keep in mind, though, that this statement doesn't need to be lengthy. Instead, create a concise statement that explains how you want to be remembered as a leader.

Now, though, it's time to learn about the *MinddogTV* podcast in chapter ten.

CHAPTER 10
MINDDOGTV

Matt Nappo is the creator of the *Minddog TV* podcast. Although, this is an unusual name for a podcast, Nappo interviews amazing guests on his show. The best way to learn about Nappo's podcast is for me to tell you about some of the episodes.

So, let's start by learning about networking, with a lady who is an expert on this topic. If this sounds interesting to you, the interview with Jen Nash took place on November 30, 2021.

Although it's important for people in business to network, many people are frightened to do this because most people don't like talking to strangers. Even Nappo admits that he doesn't like talking to people he doesn't know.

However, sometimes you need to learn how to do new things if you want to make more money. Indeed, when you start talking to people, you will start learning about new business opportunities. Doesn't that sound great?

According to Nash you aren't going to make connections with other people by staying at home. By now, you're probably wondering, "What would I say to a stranger?" In fact, just thinking about this question might prevent you from talking to other people.

The good news, though, is that you don't need to be a clever conversationalist before you get started with networking. Indeed, Nash suggests making small talk to break the ice. So even when you're standing next to a cheese tray at a refreshment table, use this as a networking opportunity

If Nash was standing next to the cheese tray, she would know exactly what to say. Although, this might sound obvious, Nash would tell everyone how much she enjoys Gouda cheese.

Do you see how simple this is? To be honest, if you approach networking in the right way, it doesn't need to be difficult at all. Of course, I need to keep telling myself this because I am interested in connecting with other people, so this is a topic I need to take more seriously.

Something else to be aware of, is that Nash has written a book about networking. So, for those who are interested, her book is titled *The Big Power Of Tiny Connections*. Indeed, I have just started reading this book and have already learned a lot.

Now, for something completely different, let's learn about artificial intelligence. There is a fellow named Mo Gawdat who used to be an important person at Google. However, even though Gawdat was successful in the business world, he wasn't happy.

Then, in 2014, Gawdat's world was turned upside down when his son died. Of course, Gawdat's son meant everything to him, and he still thinks about their conversations. Interestingly enough, though, in many ways his son had been his teacher. Before we go any further, this interview took place on September 22, 2022.

Recently, though, Gawdat wrote a book titled *Scary Smart*. In this book Gawdat shares his ideas about artificial intelligence. But you can also learn about Gawdat's ideas in this podcast episode.

To be honest, it's a bit overwhelming when Gawdat talks about the latest developments in artificial intelligence. Although many people are frightened by this new technology, Gawdat believes artificial intelligence will improve our lives.

Something to be aware of, though, is that artificial intelligence is already smarter than we are. In fact, in the future, what we know will seem like a fly in comparison to AI. In other words, AI is no longer simply something in a science fiction movie.

Of course, Matt Nappo became concerned when he heard Gawdat say this. Indeed, Nappo began worrying about whether AI was going to kill or enslave us. However, Gawdat doesn't believe we should be afraid of AI.

Instead, he believes it's not too late to teach AI about ethics. Although this might seem like an impossible task,

Gawdat thinks ordinary people can accomplish. By now, you're probably wondering, "How do we do this?"

According to Gawdat, we need to show AI that people aren't as bad as they often appear to be. To make a long story short, not everybody is as bad as Adolf Hitler. Thankfully, there are many good people in the world.

However, AI will never learn about the good things happening if people only post negative things on the Internet. Although I'm skeptical of Gawdat's theory, I certainly hope he is right.

After listening to Gawdat during this interview I wanted to learn more about this interesting man. So, I read some articles about him, and I also began listening to his *Slo Mo* podcast. In fact, I enjoyed listening to Gawdat's podcast so much, that his show will be the topic of the next chapter.

Although, we have just learned about the future, now it's time to learn about the past. Indeed, a fellow named Guy Windsor just happens to be an expert in medieval swordsmanship. Of course, when Nappo learned about Windsor, he asked him to be a guest on his podcast.

So, for those who are interested, this interview took place on September 28, 2021. Although Nappo knows very little about medieval swordsmanship, he quickly discovers that it's kind of a big deal.

In fact, Nappo learns from Windsor that medieval swordsmanship is more popular in America than it is in Europe. At first, Nappo finds this hard to believe until Windsor insists it is true. Of course, it's hard to argue with the fact that Windsor sells most of his books and online courses to Americans.

Although Windsor is from England, he also lived for a while in Finland. The most important thing to know about Windsor, though, is that he loves teaching people about medieval swordsmanship. Indeed, when you listen to him talk about this topic, you will also want to learn more about it.

Something to be aware of, though, is that medieval swordsmanship can become an expensive hobby. For example, a good sword costs $300, and a custom-made sword costs much more than that. Once you become interested in this hobby, you will probably want to buy more than one sword.

Then, after you buy your sword, you will need to learn how to use it. Of course, when you own a deadly weapon, safety is the most important thing. Thankfully, though, most sword enthusiasts never get seriously injured. However, when you're fighting with other people, you may get some bruises.

Windsor suggests doing some exercises such as push-ups, so you have the strength in your arms to take your swordsmanship to the next level. Although, it might not seem like it, swinging a sword and wearing armor is exhausting.

Unfortunately, during the pandemic, it was difficult for medieval swordsmanship enthusiasts to gather together.

Windsor realized this was a problem and decided to write a book about practicing swordsmanship by yourself.

Hopefully it won't be long before people can gather together in their swordsmanship clubs. In fact, I did some research and discovered there is a medieval swordsmanship club in my area. So, don't be surprised if you see me swinging a sword around.

Now let's learn about disasters, in an interview that takes place on June 2, 2021. Before this interview, Nappo admitted that he was nervous about interviewing David Dodd. However, there was no need for Nappo to worry since he did a great job of interviewing his guest.

Sadly, many disasters happen throughout this world. For example, when Hurricane Katrina hit New Orleans, it did quite a bit of damage. Thankfully, though, after this disaster happened, a lot of money was spent to protect New Orleans from future hurricanes.

Of course, it would have been better if common sense precautions had taken place before Katrina hit. Unfortunately, though, human nature often prevents communities and companies from preparing for disasters since people are hesitant to spend money preparing for something that might not happen. Dodd, though, believes that preparing for disasters is similar to buying life insurance. Although you may want to live forever, you buy life insurance to protect your family.

The nice thing about preparing for disasters is that it doesn't always have to cost a lot of money. For example, just storing several extra cans of food in your cupboard, could make a big difference. So, stop thinking about preparing yourself, and start doing it.

However, after you have prepared yourself, it's time to think about other people. Indeed, you're not going to be happy if you see your neighbors suffering.

You won't know how to help your neighbors if you have never met them. So, spend some time and find out which people in your neighborhood are going to need your help during a disaster.

As you can see, there is a lot of valuable information in this interview. In fact, this information is so important that I'm hoping you will listen to this podcast episode.

Now that you have learned how to protect yourself from disasters, it's time to learn about creativity. Although, I know a little bit about this topic, it's Maria Brito who is the real creativity expert. Nappo interviewed her on March 16, 2022.

The first thing you need to know is that everyone is creative. Although, you might not feel creative, both Brito and Nappo think you are. So, even though it might be hard to believe, you are a creative person.

However, being creative, doesn't mean you need to become a famous painter, sculptor, or writer. This is good news, because it means there are many different ways you can express your creativity.

Sometimes though, your supervisors at work don't want you to be creative. In fact, it's often a boring work routine which makes many people believe they're not creative. Interestingly enough, Brito can identify with this since she was miserable when she worked as a lawyer.

Eventually though, Brito created her own creative career. Indeed, now she visits talented artists in their studios. Constantly associating with successful painters has helped her learn more about creativity.

In fact, Brito has learned so much about creativity, that she has written a book on this topic. So, for those who are interested, her book is titled *How Creativity Rules The World*. Of course, after listening to this interview, this is another book I want to read.

This chapter is coming to an end, but in the next one we will learn about public speaking. Although speaking before a large audience is frightening to most people, this is something you can learn how to do.

Indeed, Sean Tyler Foley is someone who can teach you how to become a public speaker. In fact, not only is Foley an expert in public speaking, but he is also an actor. Although being on television and in movies is glamorous, Foley prefers speaking in front of thousands of people.

Before we go any further, Nappo interviewed Foley on March 23, 2022. During this interview, Nappo told Foley he is an introvert and that it's hard for him to speak to a small audience. He said he finds it easier to speak in front of a large audience.

Foley understands what it's like to be an introvert, since he is also an introvert. Of course, Nappo is surprised to hear this since Foley has such an outgoing personality. But Foley responds by saying after the interview with Nappo he'd be taking a nap.

If you think about this, it makes sense, since not every successful public speaker is an extrovert. In other words, don't give up on public speaking because you don't think you have the right type of personality for it.

Although the *MinddogTV* podcast is amazing, it's now time to learn about the *Slo Mo* podcast.

CHAPTER 11
SLO MO

The Slo Mo Podcast was created by Mo Gawdat. As I mentioned in the previous chapter, at one time Gawdat was an important person at Google. However, that was several years ago, so now he has moved on to other things.

Thankfully, I recently learned about the *Slo Mo* podcast. I was so fascinated with this podcast that I decided to include it in this book. So, let's get started with learning about some of the guests Gawdat has interviewed.

Have you ever wondered about what will happen in the future? Well, believe it or not, some people spend a lot of time trying to predict the future. In fact, a person who tries to predict the future is called a futurist.

Being a futurist isn't easy, though, because you have to look at a lot of data. However, there is a woman named Rebecca Costa who has been making predictions for many years. Sometimes, though, Costa says things people don't want to hear.

For example, she believes society is going to collapse. Sadly, Costa thinks this will be a global collapse. On the bright side, though, she doesn't think everyone is going to die. Of course, I'm thankful for this because I would like to live a little bit longer.

Although it's not pleasant to learn there could be tough times ahead, Costa is probably right. Interestingly enough, though, Costa believes that artificial intelligence will soften the impact of the collapse.

When I was listening to this interview, I thought Gawdat would disagree with Costa. However, during this interview which takes place on October 14, 2021, Gawdat takes her ideas seriously.

I think one of the reasons Gawdat enjoys talking with Costa, is because they're both fascinated with artificial intelligence. Although I'm not as interested in AI as they are, I must admit it's an interesting topic.

To make a long story short, though, Costa believes our world has become too complicated. One example of this complexity is that Costa can't understand what her financial planner is telling her. To me, though, this example is too anecdotal.

In other words, if Costa's financial adviser doesn't know how to communicate, then it's time for her to find a different adviser. Although this sounds like I am being a bit critical of Costa, I still agree with most of what she says. I encourage you to listen to this podcast episode so that you can form your own opinion.

Now though, it's time to learn about psychology. Fortunately, there is a lady named Britt Frank who is an expert on this topic. Gawdat interviews her on April 2, 2022.

First, let me say that Frank is easy to understand. Indeed, she is so articulate that you might forget she is highly educated. However, if you want to improve your life, Frank is the right person to listen to. So, let's start by learning how Frank helps her clients.

Sometimes when Frank is working with her clients, they become stuck and look to her for advice. Although it would be easy for Frank to tell her clients what to do, sometimes she lets them solve their own problems. In other words, most people already know what they should be doing, but they don't want to do it.

However, before you can make changes in your life, you need to be honest with yourself. Indeed, even if you don't want to change anything, you still should be honest with yourself.

Unfortunately, some of the people Frank tries to help really don't want to be helped. This makes Frank sad because she genuinely wants to help other people. However, she realizes that some people aren't ready to improve their lives.

In fact, when Frank was younger, she had a lot of problems. Although it wasn't easy, eventually she learned how to become honest with herself. In other words, she began to realize when she was full of crap.

Now the biggest problem Frank has is that she is a workaholic. However, since she knows this is a problem, she is already trying to correct it. So, as you can see, Frank is someone who practices what she preaches.

It's time to move on to a new topic. In fact, it's time to learn how to do you. Although, it might be hard to believe, Jacqueline Hurst is an expert in this topic and wrote a book that explains how to do you. Gawdat interviews Hurst on February 12, 2022.

According to Hurst, the first thing you need learn is that you're already good enough. Sadly, many people don't think they are good enough. The reason they feel this way is because they're constantly comparing themselves to others. Hurst knows about not feeling good enough because this used to be one of her problems.

Thankfully, though, through a lot of hard work, she learned that she didn't need to compare herself to others. Although learning how to feel good about yourself might seem simple, many people struggle with this.

So, even if you already feel like you're good enough, you probably know people who don't feel this way. When Hurst had this problem, she felt terrible every day. Now, though, she is a life coach and able to help others.

Although this might be hard to believe, Hurst has already worked with 8,000 clients and writes articles for GQ magazine. However, one thing she doesn't do is compete with other life coaches.

Indeed, there is no need for Hurst to do this since she doesn't spend time worrying about other people. Instead, Hurst just tries to be the best life coach she can be. Since she has plenty of clients, she must be doing something right.

To my surprise, I learned more from this interview than I thought I would. Even though I don't usually compare myself to others, I know I'm certainly not perfect. But according to Hurst, I'm already good enough.

Now it's time to learn about positive psychology. It's okay if you have never heard about this type of psychology because Robert Biswas-Denier knows all about it. In fact, Denier has written books about this topic. So, if this sounds interesting to you, this interview takes place on January 20, 2021.

The first thing you should know about Denier is that he likes to travel. However, when Denier travels to different parts of the world, he doesn't stay at fancy hotels. Instead, Denier goes on real adventures and meets poor people. Many of Denier's most exciting adventures happened when he was a young man.

Of course, since Denier has traveled to places like Greenland, India, and Kenya, he has a lot of stories to tell. He has also visited the Amish and the homeless people in America.

The reason Denier traveled so much is because he needed to figure out what makes people happy. According to Denier, it's our relationships with other people that make us happy. To be honest, this insight was surprising to me, since I would rather be a hermit.

Also, Denier discovered that money isn't as important as we think it is. So, to make a long story short, money isn't going to make you happy. Personally, I agree with Denier, and I think he is someone worth listening to.

Now, though, it's time to learn how to take it easy. Of course, this doesn't mean you should be lazy, but sometimes you need to learn how to say no. Unfortunately, Becky Morrison had to learn this lesson the hard way.

Indeed, there was a time when Morrison was a workaholic. Of course, this wasn't good because Morrison was trying to do too much. Then one day she nearly died in the hospital. Sadly, though, Morrison was still more worried about her career as a lawyer than the fact that she nearly died.

Before we go any further, this *Slo Mo* podcast episode takes place on May 5, 2021. Eventually, Morrison realized she needed to start taking care of herself. In other words, she decided to stop working so many hours.

Now, Morrison no longer works as a lawyer since that type of work wasn't making her happy. In fact, believe it or not, Morrison now works as a happiness coach. This is a much better job for her, and she enjoys helping her clients.

Interestingly enough, Morrison's husband was also a workaholic. However, eventually her husband realized he was doing too much and now he works as a high school basketball coach.

Now, for something a little bit different, how would you feel if you could spend some time by yourself? That's right. Are there times when you wish you could be alone? If you're feeling this way, don't worry, there is nothing wrong with you.

In fact, there is a lady named Francesca Specter who has written a book about being alone. If this sounds interesting to you, Gawdat interviewed Specter on July 17, 2021.

Although Specter is an extrovert, she has discovered there are times when she would rather be alone. Being alone, though, doesn't mean you have to be lonely. Indeed, if you go about it in the right way, being by yourself can be a positive experience.

For example, once a week, Specter goes to the movies by herself. Although technically there are other people in the theater, it's a bit unusual to see a movie by yourself. However, since by nature I'm a loner, this is something I have done many times.

Something else Specter likes to do by herself is go out to eat. Out of self-respect, though, Specter likes to dress nicely when she goes to a restaurant. She doesn't do this to be attractive to other people. Instead, she does this because she likes to dress up for special occasions.

You might be thinking, "This type of life is alright for Specter, but it would never work for me." However, when you think about it, the changes she suggests really aren't that drastic. In other words, Specter isn't asking you to become a hermit.

To be honest, I agree with most of the things Specter says during this interview. In fact, I was already doing many of the things she Specter recommends before I knew who she was. Although, if you really want to understand Specter's ideas, you need to listen to this podcast episode.

Unfortunately, I only have space in this chapter to tell you about one more interview, and it's with a famous economist named Yanis Varoufakis who at one time was the Greek finance minister.

Before we go any further, though, this podcast episode takes place on January 22, 2022. Of course, Gawdat was thrilled to interview Varoufakis since this is someone he really admires. Indeed, the reason he admires him is because Varoufakis is a brave man.

For those who don't know, several years ago, Greece was in the middle of a financial crisis. Although Varoufakis didn't think of himself as a politician, he agreed to run for office. So, to make a long story short, Varoufakis ended up becoming the finance minister of Greece.

Sadly, during the Greek financial crisis, many people suffered. Greedy bankers didn't care about what happened to the people of Greece. Thankfully, though, Varoufakis tried to make things better for his country.

Needless to say, the greedy bankers hated Varoufakis because he wouldn't cooperate with them. So, in 2015, Varoufakis had an epic battle with the bankers. Although, this was an exciting interview with Yanis Varoufakis, it's now time to move on to chapter twelve. Are you ready?

CHAPTER 12
WHAT'S ESSENTIAL

Greg McKeown created the *What's Essential* podcast. If McKeown's name sounds familiar, it's because I talked about him in the fourth chapter of this book. At the time I wrote that chapter, though, I knew very little about his podcast.

However, in the past few weeks I have been listening to the *What's Essential* podcast and I'm very impressed with it. So, let me tell you about some of the interviews because I know you're going to love McKeown's podcast.

To begin with, let's learn how ancient wisdom can improve your life. Indeed, since I'm fascinated with ancient philosophy, I'm glad McKeown interviewed Ryan Holiday. If this topic sounds interesting to you, this interview takes place on August 17, 2020.

Stoic philosophy helped Holiday understand himself and the world around him. In case you don't know, Stoicism is a type of philosophy that was popular in ancient times. However, people such as Holiday believe we can still learn valuable lessons from the past.

For example, one of the ancient philosophers Holiday admires is Seneca. Although I don't consider myself a Stoic, I do admire Seneca. Since Seneca was a deep thinker, sometimes he wrote things people did not want to hear.

Indeed, one insight Seneca had is that people waste a lot of time. To be honest, not only do people waste a lot of time, then they say life is too short. However, Seneca says that life wouldn't be too short if people spent their time wisely.

Of course, I have to agree with Seneca since what he says makes so much sense. Sadly, though, it's quite easy to spend your time doing things that really aren't important. The good news, though, is that you can improve your life if you listen to Seneca.

Although, if you're not interested in Seneca, Holiday also talks about how much he enjoys being a father. Indeed, Holiday loves to go on long walks with his children. He also likes to pick blackberries. In other words, there is something for everyone in this interview.

Have you heard of FOMO? For those who don't know, FOMO stands for fear of missing out. Interestingly enough, this term was invented by Patrick McGininnis when he was a college student.

In fact, the reason McGinnis invented this term was because he was always worried that he would miss out on something.

Of course, McGinnis isn't the only person who has to deal with FOMO. Indeed, this term has become so popular that now you can find FOMO in the dictionary. Although it was an honor to have FOMO placed in the dictionary, McGinnis wants to be remembered for more than this.

To be honest, McGinnis should be remembered for more than this since he is an important person in the business world. In fact, not only did McGinnis attend Harvard Business School, but he has also written useful business books. Before we go any further, though, McKeown interviews McGinnis on July 20, 2020.

One of the books McGinnis wrote is called *The 10% Entrepreneur.* Although, I haven't read this book, it's supposed to be helpful for people who want to become entrepreneurs. If this sounds frightening to you, don't worry, you won't have to quit your day job.

Instead, McGinnis recommends becoming a part-time entrepreneur. This makes sense because then you can gradually learn what you need to know. In other words, starting a side hustle isn't as risky as becoming a full-time entrepreneur.

Of course, this doesn't mean you can't eventually become a full-time entrepreneur. However, what's the point in putting pressure on yourself, when all you have is an interesting business idea. Although, if you have your heart set on starting out as a full-time entrepreneur, that's alright too.

As you can see, McGinnis is knowledgeable about the business world. Indeed, I have to admit that I was impressed with the things he said. So, I encourage you to listen to this podcast episode.

Are you someone who spends too much time overthinking things? I know I sometimes do. Thankfully, though, Jon Acuff is an expert on this topic. In fact, Acuff has even written a book about this topic which is titled *Soundtracks*.

Before we go any further, this podcast episode takes place on April 19, 2021. Of course, McKeown is happy to interview Acuff since both men are interested in similar things. For example, at one point in the interview McKeown says that he would like to work on a project with Acuff.

To be honest, I was excited to listen to this interview since I'm currently reading one of Acuff's earlier books. In case you're curious, the book I'm reading is titled *Finish*. In other words, I will need to finish the book *Finish* before I can read *Soundtracks*.

When I first heard the title, *Soundtracks*, I thought it was an odd title for a book. However, now that I understand what Acuff's book is about, it makes more sense.

According to Acuff, we all have soundtracks playing inside our mind. The problem is that these soundtracks are often quite negative. Not only that, but sometimes our soundtracks aren't even true.

For example, sometimes people say they want to exercise. When Acuff suggests something fun in the way of exercise,

most people don't like his advice. Right now, you're probably wondering, "What do people have against fun?"

Sadly, many people believe they have to be miserable before they can get any benefit from exercising. Of course, the
negative soundtrack playing inside their mind isn't true. In
fact, not only is this soundtrack not true, but it is also actually quite silly.

Another problem many people have is that they overthink
things. Unfortunately, quite often people don't realize they
have this problem. Instead, they will say that they are detail-oriented. So, how do you know if you really are detail-
oriented?

Acuff says the answer is that detail-oriented people actually
know how to get things done. So, if you never seem to finish any of your projects, you're probably overthinking
things. If this is the case, though, don't get discouraged.

Instead, just realize that you need to change the soundtrack
playing inside your mind. Of course, this type of transfor-
mation will take some time, so I recommend listening to
this entire interview.

The next person I want to tell you about is a famous *Ted
Talks* speaker. In fact, Simon Sinek is the third most popular speaker *Ted Talks* has ever had. This is saying a lot when
you consider all the people who have given Ted Talks.

Interestingly enough, though, not only is Sinek a public
speaker, but he is also a talented writer. Indeed, for those

who don't know, Sinek is the author of *Start With Why*. In this book, Sinek talks about successful people such as Steve Jobs and Martin Luther King, Jr.

Of course, it would have been easy for Sinek to continue writing books similar to *Start With Why*. However, since Sinek is a creative person, this isn't what he chose to do. Instead, Sinek ignored the advice of his publishers and wrote the books he wanted to write.

If this sounds interesting to you, this interview takes place on November 1, 2021. Personally, I think that McKeown does a great job of interviewing Sinek. For example, McKeown discovers that Sinek thinks of himself as an optimist.

Although optimism means nothing to me, for some reason it's important to Sinek. However, what I do like about Sinek is that he is a deep thinker. Indeed, Sinek has even spent a lot of time trying to figure out how the Wright Brothers invented the airplane.

To make a long story short, the Wright Brothers didn't have much money, but they still outsmarted their rivals. Of course, if you want to benefit from Sinek's wisdom, then you will need to listen to this interview.

Have you ever worried that you spend too much time working? If this is the case, you're going to love the next interview with Michael Hyatt. Although Michael Hyatt used to be a workaholic, he eventually realized he was trying to do too much.

Indeed, it was Hyatt's wife who told him he was working too much. When he saw his wife crying, he decided to be a better husband. Not only that, Hyatt also realized he needed to spend more time with his children.

Before we go any further, this interview takes place on March 1, 2021. As you can see from Hyatt's story, it's important to live a balanced life. In other words, what good is it to work long hours if it's destroying your family?

When you work fewer hours, though, you need to learn how to set priorities. Indeed, the reason you need to set priorities is because much of the work you're doing isn't necessary.

For example, Hyatt decided to reduce the hours his employees worked, but he still paid them the same amount of money. What do you think happened? The answer is that his workers accomplished more in thirty hours than they had when they worked forty hours.

So how did Hyatt's workers do this? They did it by only doing work that was absolutely essential. To be honest, it didn't bother Hyatt to pay his workers the same amount even though they were working fewer hours.

In fact, it made Hyatt happy, because he enjoyed seeing his workers spending more time with their families. Sadly, though, not all bosses are as kind as Hyatt. However, to be fair, it did take him a while to get his act together.

The good news is that you can still prioritize what you do when you're not working. For example, although I work a full-time job, I have still written five books in the past three years. Of course, your goals might be different than mine, but this doesn't mean you shouldn't have priorities.

I'm sad to say it, but this book is coming to an end. Fortunately, though, I still have space to tell you about a fellow named Jay Papasan. For those who don't know, Papasan was the co-author of *The One Thing*.

Although I have only browsed through *The One Thing*, this was a very popular business book. In fact, even though this book was published in 2013, people are still talking about it. So, what made this business book so fascinating?

The answer is that Gary W. Keller and Jay Papasan wrote a book that teaches people how to set priorities. Of course, *The One Thing* isn't the only book ever written on this topic. However, many people absolutely love the ideas in this book.

Before we go any further, though, McKeown interviews Papasan on November 16, 2020. According to Papasan, many of the tasks we work on really don't help us accomplish our goals. Although this makes sense, the question is, "What can we do about it?"

The answer is that we need to figure out the one thing we can do that will help us accomplish our goals. Interestingly enough, Papasan insists this one thing must be something we can do right now.

Of course, this doesn't mean that one thing is your only priority. Indeed, Papasan realizes that people have many important priorities in their busy lives. However, your one thing is something you're focusing on right now.

For example, if you're reading a book to a child, don't stop reading to answer the phone. Although this sounds like common sense advice, it's certainly something I need to work on.

Another example Papasan gives is that he needs to be kind to his wife on their date night. Indeed, the way Papasan shows respect for her is by not looking at the sports scores when they're at the restaurant.

As you can tell by what I have told you about Papasan, he is a very wise man.

CONCLUSION

If you have read this far, I guarantee you have learned a lot about the best podcasts on the Internet. Although, to be honest, I have also learned quite a bit by writing this book. Indeed, I needed to listen to quite a few podcasts to find the best ones for you.

When I was writing this book many people told me they didn't listen to podcasts. In fact, there were even some people who told me they didn't know anything about podcasts. However, if you have finished reading this book, you already know more about podcasts than most people.

Something you need to be aware of, though, is that the podcasting world is constantly changing. For example, when I was writing the last chapter of this book, I discussed the *What's Essential* podcast.

Sadly, before I finished writing the chapter, the podcast's name changed. So now if you want to listen to this podcast you need to enter Greg McKeown into the Stitcher search engine.

Although, there is a lot of information in this book, there is one more thing you need to know. I'm a hermit. However, if you happen to meet me, I will be happy to sign your book.

ACKNOWLEDGEMENTS

Here is a list of people that I would like to thank:

Marcie Morgan, Samantha Ballard, David Ballard, Mariela Harris, Jackie Smith, Ryan Smith, Lisa Smith, Casi Smith, Marcia Meade, Carla Hill, Jason Alexander, Tahy Alvin, Nathan Nelson, Michael Davis, Andrew Lines, Lorie Christopherson, Dina Caine, Stephanie Blank, Jonathan Love, and Marissa Orme.

Made in the USA
Middletown, DE
22 December 2022

16839706R00073